Sept. 1957.

THE SIGNS OF OUR TIMES

Other books by the same author

*

Family Circle (a study of the Epworth Household)
John Wesley and the Eighteenth Century
After Wesley
Methodism and England (1850–1932)
This Methodism
Adam Clarke
S. E. Keeble
Church and Society
One Increasing Purpose (Beckley Lecture 1947)
So Rich a Crown
etc.

THE SIGNS
OF OUR TIMES

The Cato Lecture of 1957

BY

MALDWYN EDWARDS

M.A., B.D. (Cantab), M.A. (Wales), Ph.D. (London)

LONDON

THE EPWORTH PRESS

THE EPWORTH PRESS
(FRANK H. CUMBERS)
25-35 City Road, London, E.C. 1

MELBOURNE   CAPE TOWN
NEW YORK   TORONTO

PRINTED IN GREAT BRITAIN BY ROBERT MACLEHOSE AND CO. LTD
THE UNIVERSITY PRESS, GLASGOW

TO
DAVID MICHAEL
my grandson

PREFACE

I AM very sensible of the honour of being invited to deliver the Cato Lecture. It has given me the opportunity to develop a line of thought which has interested me for many years. The essay comes within the field of Church History and more particularly within the concern of the Church with social ethics. The first part is a short historical survey of Renaissance and post-Renaissance thinking about man. Then follows an examination of contemporary thought and movements under the light of Christian principles. Finally in three chapters on the relevance of the Bible, the Church, and Christian teaching on the Last Things, I have sought to show the relevance of the Christian Faith for the needs of modern man.

I should like to acknowledge with deep gratitude the help of Mrs Valerie Morgan who has typed the manuscript, and of my son-in-law, the Rev. Brian Greet, who has prepared the Index and seen the book through the Press. I am also greatly indebted to Dr H. G. Wood and the Rev. Dr E. Benson Perkins, who read the manuscript, and made wise and helpful observations.

Once again I am conscious of the great debt I owe to the unfailing kindness and assistance of the Book Steward and Editor of the Epworth Press. In particular I should like Frank Cumbers to know of my deep sense of obligation to him since he became Book Steward. Were I not proudly dedicating the book to my first grandchild I should like to have offered it to him.

Even before I leave for Australia to deliver the Lecture, I am indebted to those who have arranged an itinerary for me and made such thorough preparations. In this connexion I am most grateful to the Rev. Dr H. G. Seccomb and the Rev. Dr Harold Wood. Their essential friendliness can be felt even through their correspondence. Through them I realize more than ever the privilege of serving the great Methodist Church in Australia.

Finally, now as always, I should like to thank my family circle, and particularly my wife, for sustained interest in the preparation of the book. My wife has always believed I should find time to write the book and because of that, it has been done.

MALDWYN EDWARDS

CONTENTS

INTRODUCTION

A précis of the argument of this book

THE collapse of the medieval solidarity of Church and Empire meant the emergence both of national States and of individualism in religion. A new significance was given to man. Even the great Reformers could not wholly withstand the thought movements of their age. The sixteenth-century emphasis on religion became in the seventeenth century a concern with metaphysics. The rationalism of the following century gave place in the nineteenth century to a stress on economics. Our present century has been called 'The scientific age' and attention is focused on men's technical achievements. Throughout the whole of this period, however, there has been unabated confidence in man's capacity to go forward into his golden age.

It was only in August 1914 that the first misgivings were clearly heard. In the subsequent thirty years of war, unemployment, terror, and a second total war, the process of disillusionment finally settled into despair. The Renaissance conception of man had finally proved its falsity; an old order had ended. The humanists are still with us, but the facts of history and human nature have broken down their over-cheerful hypothesis. The one philosophy of human nature which has been vindicated by events is the Christian doctrine of original sin. Man was made in the image of God but the image has been defaced. He is not able therefore to achieve his destiny unaided. We are thrown back upon a theology of grace. In the divine economy God and man must work together.

Man lives, however, within the politically organized State. In the light of Christian principles what form must that take? Neither an individualist nor a State democracy is a sufficient answer. Both have advantages which are nullified by grievous shortcomings. Even a social democracy must be appraised by certain canons of judgement and its limits must be clearly recognized. There is a Christian critique of the State which is understood most clearly when the Communist theory of the State is passed under review. The Communist life-and-death challenge can only be met confidently by those who understand the true Christian basis of democratic government. Without that knowledge we are men of straw.

But we are not only citizens of a State; we are members of society. There are not wanting indications that order in society is being recovered. After the moral nihilism of the thirties and forties, the present decade may be called the decade of discovery. In ecology, in science, in psychology, and the study of history, there is a recognition that we are not part of the fertile spawn of nature, thrown blindly on the shores of time. These sciences are concerned with a description of the earth, with man in relation to his natural environment, with the structure of man's mind and with the story of his past. They are therefore of essential importance in showing a drift toward the concepts of order, purpose, and the moral bias of the created world. This in turn predicates a return to a spiritual interpretation of life and a God whose will cannot be resisted with impunity.

Nevertheless this return to holiness and sanity needs still to be worked out in the four great areas of human activity. There must be a return to moral order in the family, in education, in industry, and in leisure and community life. We need to realize afresh in all these fields the direct bearing of Christian social ethics upon our daily life.

Have we an inspired word to speak to men in this modern situation? The dynamic inspiration of the Bible after a hundred years of intense criticism is more firmly established than ever. It speaks with unequalled authority to the condition of men. In its drama of man's redemption it has a message which is always contemporary. Here is the true inner philosophy of man's pilgrimage on earth.

But is the Church itself matched with the hour and alive to its opportunities? Despite 'our unhappy divisions' the Church is more conscious than ever of its essential oneness in Christ. We are witnessing a great movement of the Holy Spirit, which manifests itself in organic unions and in ecumenical enterprise. The need is not for strait-jacketed uniformity, but for a unity of spirit which will find its own appropriate forms of expression.

Finally, how do the aspirations of modern man appear in the light of Christian teaching on the Last Things? The Christian does not believe in blue-prints for Utopia. He does not accept any theory of the classless society, the visible Kingdom of man on earth. That is never his starting-point. He begins not with himself but with God. He believes that if God's sovereignty is acknowledged, if the laws of the Kingdom are obeyed, if Christ's victory over sin and death is appropriated, if divine resources are utilized, then the form of human living will manifest itself. The primary essential is a right relationship with God and our fellows; all else will follow. 'Seek ye first the Kingdom of God and His righteousness and all these things will be added unto you.'

Nevertheless, we shall never come to an age when 'every life shall

be a song' and 'all the earth is paradise'. By Christian teaching on
anti-Christ, the Second Coming, and the final Judgement, the Christian is delivered from a false despair, a false comfort, and a false
confidence. He knows he has his own appointed part to play, but he
also knows the last word lies with God. The Alpha and Omega who
began the story must also finish it.

> *He speaks at length the final word*
> *And ushers in the triumph hour.*

This is the word of the Church. It is a true and living word to dying
men.

Section I

THE DEBATE ON MAN

CHAPTER I

THE END OF AN AGE

HAMLET will stand for all time as the introspective man. He was cursed by his clear vision of the journey's end and his hesitation over the appropriate means to achieve it. Yet it was Hamlet, despising the earth as a 'sterile promontory', who yet delivered the most eloquent panegyric on man. All the Renaissance admiration of man, standing assured in his own sufficiency, guided only by the light of his own reason, is gathered up in a few staccato phrases—

> *What a piece of work is a man! How noble in reason!*
> *how infinite in faculty! in form, in moving, how express*
> *and admirable! in action how like an angel! in apprehen-*
> *sion how like a god! the beauty of the world! the paragon*
> *of animals!*

It was the same estimate of man which reflected itself in the architecture and sculpture of Brunelleschi, Alberti, Donatello, and Luca della Robbia. Both in sculpture and in painting, Leonardo da Vinci and Michaelangelo are supremely representative of their age. 'Curiosity and the desire for beauty', wrote Walter Pater, 'are the two elementary forces in Leonardo's genius.' Could not this be said, allowing for varying degrees of genius, of all great painters in the Florentine, Roman, and Venetian periods of Italian Renaissance art? Indeed this pride in man, this love of colour, this thirst for experiment shows itself as powerfully in the art of Rubens, Hals, and Velazquez. Though Rubens was Flemish and Hals Dutch, and the Spanish Velazquez came from the most Catholic of all Kingdoms, they were all the children of an age which believed in man and his limitless destiny. This idea was so novel and exciting that its roots need to be examined.

The overarching idea of the Middle Ages was the conception of the Holy Catholic Church and the Holy Roman Empire—the universal Church and its secular counterpart. That idea began to lose its hold in the middle of the thirteenth century. Even scholasticism in its attempt to codify knowledge under that one Truth taught by the Church was mentally stimulating, though the mind still flowed between banks, high and well defined. In humanism, however, the river often burst its banks. The Italian Renaissance scholars, revelling in classical literature, spoke of *litterae humaniores*; and their 'distinctively humane' scholar was one who in his appreciation of the good life claimed absolute freedom for the human reason.

Petrarch (1304–74) is the harbinger of a new age. He had an enthusiastic devotion for the literary and historical past of his country. His Italian ancestors were so real to him that in a letter to Boccaccio he argued that the likeness of a modern man to his classical model was not that of a portrait to the original, but that of a child to his father. Vespasiano da Besticci, in the same vein of thinking, wrote a book, *Illustrious Men*, in which he saw the civic virtues of ancient Rome flowering afresh in the Florence of his day.

Though Petrarch knew no Greek, he yielded to none in his reverence for Plato and anyhow it was but a short journey from Rome to Athens. During the next century, Latin and Greek texts were rediscovered. Long before the fall of Constantinople, there was contact between it and Italy through trade and theological discussion. Students studied in the libraries of Constantinople and in some cases returned with manuscripts. A Byzantine, Manuel Chrysoloras, taught Greek in Florence at the end of the fourteenth century. His Greek Grammar, devised in the form of question and answer, was the first book of its kind, and throughout the next century, Florence was the most vigorous centre of Greek studies. The fall of Constantinople did not therefore introduce Greek thought to the West, but it quickened a process already well begun.

If Renaissance scholars had had this heritage alone, they might have learnt from the ancients the weary cycle of history and the tears at the heart of the things. They were saved from a melancholy, ending in despair, because they were also heirs of the Christian Hope. In the Middle Ages the individual might seem to be lost within the ecclesiastical hierarchy, but no one doubted that he was a child of God capable of damnation or eternal blessedness.

Doubtless, as Platonists, Aristotelians, and Stoics affirmed, he had νοῦς (rationality), but since he was living within a supernatural order, there was no need to prophesy doom. Indeed his origin and equipment combined to magnify his person and to push impatiently aside any limits to his aspirations. Miranda in *The Tempest* spoke for more than herself when she cried:

> *O, wonder!*
> *How many goodly creatures are there here!*
> *How beauteous mankind is! O brave new world,*
> *That has such people in 't !*

It is true that the Reformation strove to correct an unduly optim-istic view of man's nature by its insistence on original sin. Neither Luther nor Calvin was in any doubt concerning the fallen nature of mankind. Yet despite this starkly realistic judgement on man the Renaissance conception triumphed. Some day someone will work out the effects of the social environment of an age upon its religious think-ing, and when that highly necessary and important work of research is done, it will be found that the Reformation was largely conditioned by the thought-forms of the Renaissance. After all, the world had known of Christopher Columbus's discovery of a new world for twenty-five years when the theses of Luther were nailed to the Cathedral door at Wittenberg. Before the close of that century, the Cabots had dis-covered Newfoundland and Labrador, and Vasco da Gama had sailed to India. Erasmus had already published his *Praise of Folly*, exposing ecclesiastics to the same scathing criticism as that accorded to laymen. When monks at the last Judgement spoke of their duties performed on earth, Christ replied: 'There is only one law which is truly mine, and of that I hear nothing.' Nicholas of Cusa had already contradicted ideas of Aristotle and Ptolemy and spoken of a moving world. In 1543 Copernicus was to publish *De Revolutionibus Orbium Coelestium* and thereby point to the sun rather than the earth as the centre of the uni-verse. And Galileo was still further to revolutionize men's thinking. George Bernard Shaw made the Bishop of Beauvais say with great prescience: 'As a priest I have gained a knowledge of the minds of the common people; and there you will find yet another most dangerous idea. I can express it only by such phrases as France for the French, England for the English, Italy for the Italians, Spain for the Spanish.... To her [Joan] the French-speaking people are what the Holy Scrip-tures describe as a nation. Call this side of her heresy Nationalism if you will: I can find you no better name for it. I can only tell you that it is essentially anti-Catholic and anti-Christian; for the Catholic Church knows only one realm, and that is the realm of Christ's kingdom.' When Henry VIII of England and Francis I of France met on the Field of the Cloth of Gold (1530), all the Bishop's fears were justified. The very title of their meeting-place symbolized most fittingly the pride of Renaissance monarchs, flushed in their new-found glory. Together with Charles V, crowned Emperor the previous year, they were the political inheritors of the new age. Already their apology had been written by Machiavelli. In *The Prince*, written in 1513, he divorced the art of government entirely from the authority of the Church. The State was not an instrument of religion, but on the contrary religion could be an instrument of the State. Politics was separated from ethics and made an end in itself. The Prince need be guided by no other considerations than the strengthening of his own authority.

Only a year before the startled Cathedral authorities pounced upon the ninety-five theses, Sir Thomas More's *Utopia* had carried in its very title the limitless aspirations of this brave new world. More, as a good Catholic, had much sympathy with monastic communism. Nevertheless his Utopians practised a natural unsectarian religion which was essentially personal and only caused State intervention when fanaticism produced disorder. In separating religion from politics, More was very much a child of his age.

Most important feature of all was the quickly emerging interest in Science. The new world discoveries in plants as well as rocks quickened this impulse. Da Vinci's anatomical studies, and the researches of Vesalius marked a new and scientific approach to the structure of the human body. Campanella, despite his tortures and imprisonment, could still wax eloquent over the new inventions of 'typography, the cannon, and the mariner's compass'. As he pertinently remarked, more books had been published in the first Renaissance century than in 'the previous four thousand years'.

Inevitably the man of Luther's day was not unlike the Balboa (Keats confuses him with Cortez) whose actual exploits took place in the same period. The rolling waters of the Pacific had come into view. The old world lay behind. He was 'silent on a peak in Darien'. Now the Reformer is in many respects the most conservative of men, and both Luther and Calvin in many respects stood rock-like in a sea of change. Luther's work on the depravity of natural man (*De Servo Arbitrio*) was an unqualified statement of human guilt and the absence of any virtue. God, it is true, is the gracious Father ready to forgive and receive those who, not trusting in any merit of their own, freely commit themselves to Him by faith alone. Yet apart from Christ a man could only know the severity of God visiting him justly in wrath. There was no concession here to the spirit of the age. '*Sola gratia sola fide*' is not a Renaissance formula.

Nevertheless, by his stand, Luther unconsciously strengthened in some respects the prevailing view of man. This was shown in three main respects. First of all, in his defiance of papal authority he was breaking free from the solidarity of medieval life and practice. Assert the right of a man to appropriate God's grace by his own act of faith, and in the process of time comes individualism in religion. The next century might bring all religious controversy to the arbitrament of the sword, and even after the Thirty Years War leave only to Princes the right to decide what form of Christian Faith to choose. But '*cuius regio eius religio*' was obviously only a temporary compromise. Men who were ready to suffer and die for their religion were not prepared to leave their conscience in the safe custody of their Prince. In the eighteenth century, Methodism would not only assert God's universal offer, but as a corollary, the fact that the 'vilest offender may turn and find grace'. It would call men to be assured of their forgiveness and of their new standing with God. In its teaching on sanctification it would offer certain parallels with the perfectibility of the individual so eloquently argued by eighteenth-century philosophers. Before Tom Paine proclaimed the rights of man in society, John Wesley had asserted those rights of man in religion. The Methodists might call a man a worm, but they went on to say: 'He calls a worm His friend.' The end of the eighteenth century was the triumph of democracy not only in political thinking but also in religious thinking. Man had come into his own not only in the sight of his fellows, but in the sight of God.

Secondly, Luther was driven by sheer force of circumstance quite as much as by temperament into a dependence upon rulers. Frightened by the extreme radicalism of some of his followers, he stressed the sin of rebellion. When the Peasants' War broke out, he called out in a famous phrase for severest measures to be taken to subdue the rebels. From the standpoint of political realism he was right. There was not the smallest chance of success. In a mundane sense, the only hope for Lutheranism in its early years was in the protection and help of the Princes. Nevertheless the price to be paid was heavy. Always Luther went back to Paul's teaching in Romans 13, forgetting that such a statement was made in certain circumstances and at a certain period in the Empire's relation with the Church; it is certain that Paul would have spoken with more qualification had he written during the persecution of Domitian. In the New Testament is also the political philosophy of the writer of the Revelation! The State might be a servant of God, but it might also in the abuse of its power become the 'Beast'. Luther believed the Prince's authority to be divinely given, but if this be granted, where can its bounds be set? He wrote to the princes on one occasion: 'It will not help the peasants to claim (Genesis 1 and 2) that all things were created free and common and that they are equally baptized. . . . For in the New Testament Moses counts for nothing; but there stands our Master Christ and casts us with body and possession under the Kaisers and worldly law when he says "Give unto Caesar the things that are Caesar's".' Luther wished to give primacy to the rights of the congregation, but the Treaty of Augsburg in 1555 showed how the alliance with the secular authority had worked to the rulers' advantage.

The distinction between the heavenly kingdom and the earthly leads to that type of otherworldliness which denies even the proximate good to be achieved in organized society. Fundamentally it despairs of the political instrument man can use, and therefore it is pessimistic in its conclusions. It is never here but always hereafter that man is truly to be blessed. To that degree the political consequences of Luther's division of the kingdoms have been disastrous. The State is only too ready to hand over the religious sphere to the Church if elsewhere it can enjoy untrammelled authority in the ordering of men's lives.

Some rulers who embraced the Lutheran faith had genuine religious convictions, but all were quick to appreciate the double advantage of freedom from ecclesiastical control, and an unearned halo in exercising their princely rights. Their use of power was given religious sanction. What could be better? Because in the Reformation the Church could not effectively be the conscience of the community, calling prince and peasant alike to their utter dependence on God and their responsibility to Him, it was a preservative neither against State tyranny nor against human pride. The dykes were far too feeble to hold back the seas of Renaissance humanism; so the defences easily broke down and the waters flooded the land. Rulers were but the children of their age, and gave their prestige to prevailing fashions of thought. Partly because of outside forces and partly because of its own inadequate political thinking, Lutheranism was therefore unable to change the fast-flowing currents of the age.

This can be illustrated in a third and last respect. One most important aspect of Luther's teaching was on the stature of the Christian man. He argued in his famous work, *The Liberty of a Christian man*, that 'as regards kingship, every Christian is by faith so exalted above all things, that in spiritual power he is completely lord of all, so that nothing whatever can do him hurt. . . . Who then can comprehend the loftiness of that Christian dignity which by its royal power rules over all things, even over death, life, and sin.' He affirmed that through faith in Christ the Christian became 'most free lord of all and subject to none'. Always Luther knew the downward drag of human appetites, and always, therefore, he knew that the grace of God was alone sufficient to secure his freedom and give him power. 'Oh faith', he said in his introduction to the Epistle to the Romans, 'is a living busy active mighty thing', and only through this faith in God's grace could a man know the freedom which replaces servitude, the love which casts out fear. Luther's man stands unshackled by bondage to any Church control, as Luther did himself when he confronted the Emperor at the Diet of Worms and declared: 'My conscience is bound to the word of God, and it is neither safe nor honest to act against one's conscience. God help me! Amen.'

This teaching has immeasurably enriched the thought of man. Nevertheless it is easy to understand how in a Renaissance world the conception could be secularized. The picture of man in dignity and freedom was eagerly seized, but the requirements for such noble liberty were easily forgotten. In time men took Luther's delineation of a man in Christ and applied it to every child of Adam.

Calvin stands with Luther as the outstanding architect of the Reformation. Although none expressed more forcibly God's transcendent majesty and man's utter depravity, yet Calvin also made unwittingly a vital contribution to the Renaissance view of man's inestimable worth. Rudyard Kipling has given us in *McAndrew's Hymn* a vivid impression of the extraordinary influence of John Calvin's *Institutes of Religion*.

> *From coupler-flange to spindle-guide I see Thy Hand, O God—*
> *Predestination in the stride o' yon connectin'-rod.*
> *John Calvin might ha' forged the same—enorrmous, certain, slow—*
> *Ay, wrought it in the furnace-flame—my 'Institutio'.*

He declared that by His own eternal and immutable counsel God had elected some to grace and predestined others to condemnation. The one case is an illustration of His infinite mercy and the other of His inflexible justice. Strangely enough, this terrifying doctrine did not have the consequences one would have anticipated. It did not produce a sense of fatalism and despair. Just as no soldier in battle can believe it is he who will be killed, so no Calvinist could believe it was he who would be damned. Cowper is a notable exception. He spoke of himself as 'the stricken deer'. In certain moods of melancholy he could be tortured by doubt, but he was sensitive and introspective to a rare degree. The Calvinists who made such excellent soldiers in Holland, Scotland, or England, were not so troubled. They knew themselves to be the object of God's favour, secure in time and in eternity. No wonder they fought well and died bravely.

In another sense Calvin contributed to the emerging picture of man's greatness. A whole school of writers, in which Max Weber and R. H.

Tawney are the best-known names, has shown the vital relation of Calvinism to the rise of trade and commerce. The contrast between the Middle Ages and the Reformation can be too tightly drawn. As Professor Tawney has indicated, there were forms of capitalism flourishing in medieval Italy and Flanders, and the spirit of capitalism was all too familiar even to 'saints and sages' in that period.[1] The overseas growth of Spain and Portugal showed strongly-emphasized economic aspects, and when the new age was emerging, it was Catholic bankers who were the leading financiers.

On the other hand, the Reformers must not be construed as encouraging a new acquisitiveness. In his tract on *Trade and Usury*, Martin Luther attacked the love of gold, and urged instead a love of neighbour in which each bears the other's burdens. Even Calvin sought to regulate all community life by Christian standards and Geneva under his rule was virtually a theocracy. Nevertheless it was Calvinism with its urban background that accepted the new world of commerce and large-scale finance. Calvin might strive to limit the excesses of usury but he did accept it. This fact alone separates him both from the medievalists and Luther himself.

The Calvinist virtues of thrift, industry, and sobriety, were excellent incentives to the rising business and trading classes of society. They had proved economic worth. The poor became rich, and the rich became richer still. Even more important was the aura of religious respectability shed on this aspect of life. The man of business could feel that in his serious application of time and energy to his own affairs he was offering a service to God. His business life was an expression of his Christian faith. It could even be interwoven with the doctrine of predestination, for success was a sign of God's election and failure could be interpreted as a sign of his reprobation. Mr V. H. H. Green (in his *Renaissance and Reformation*) has quoted with effect a translation of Tyndale: 'And God was with Joseph and he was a lucky fellow.' Dr Percy Scholes has forcibly attacked the view that Calvinism was antagonistic to the arts; but even so, the disciplined and austere approach to life stressed the overwhelming importance of worship, home, and work, and left little room for the wider reaches of cultivated living.

Calvin strove to make life difficult for the rich. He knew his New Testament too well to be indulgent to the sins of greed and covetousness and the dangers of riches. But you cannot concur in the release of a mighty torrent and then dictate its path. Puritan writers might,

---

[1] *Religion and the Rise of Capitalism*, pp. 93–5 and 112.

in the seventeenth and eighteenth centuries, deplore the tide of secularism and attack the pomp and circumstance of economic man, but Calvinism had given wealth a halo, and poverty a stigma. In time the religious reference and the religious restraints largely disappeared, but the admiration for the successful man remained.

The seventeenth century witnessed not only the wars of religion but the consequent spiritual exhaustion of man. It is significant that in Oliver Cromwell's Protectorate, religion for the last time exercised any real influence on the direction of English Foreign policy. The psalm-singing Ironsides were replaced as public figures by the courtiers who aped the manners and morals of Charles II. After the frightful exhaustion of the Thirty Years War, how easy it was to turn from so bloody an adventure in the world of religion, to a this-worldly acceptance of Louis XIV as the great ruler, and the Court of Versailles as the true centre of taste and fashion for the civilized courts of Europe. Modern man was in the making.

CHAPTER II

THE PARAGON ARRIVES

IN time, theology passed for the most part into metaphysics. Descartes worked out his philosophical system independently of scholasticism or Reformation dogma. Cartesianism rested on the proposition: '*Cogito ergo sum.*' It pressed the connexion between existence and individual consciousness. The emphasis was upon man the thinker, and even the existence of God was made consequent upon that premise. It was left to Spinoza to develop this rationalism so that God became little more than an all-embracing unifying principle, and man was left by rational inquiry to discover his own universe. Descartes founded a system of analytical geometry which in effect was the application of algebra to geometry. Spinoza used the same sort of mathematical method in exposition. He defined his axioms and then deduced his series of corollaries. It was this complete belief in reason, and in mathematics as the proper method of inquiry, which introduced the distinctive features of the modern world. Here was man, sure of his reasoning powers, and sure of his scientific outlook, ready to bring the world within the scope of his comprehension.

The eighteenth century both in England and on the Continent raised the majestic sovereign God of Luther and Calvin higher still— so high that he became the Unmoved Mover and the First Cause. Not to put too fine a point upon it, He virtually disappeared from sight. More significant still, man was promoted. Since God was an absentee landlord, the tenant could remain at will; there was not even rent to pay. Alexander Selkirk spoke for many:

> *I am monarch of all I survey;*
> *My right there is none to dispute.*
> *From the centre all round to the sea,*
> *I am lord of the fowl and the brute.*

Theologians had given place to metaphysicians and these in turn yielded their seats to the ethical and political philosophers. The supremacy of reason was acknowledged equally by Christian apologists and by their opponents. When the great Bishop Butler in his Sermons and in his *Analogy of Religion* refuted his opponents, it was to show that if they were to be consistent in their views of God, of Nature, and of Man, they must accept the Christian Faith and therefore the reasonableness of the Christian life. He did not believe in the unqualified optimism of Alexander Pope's line: 'All partial evil, universal good.' For him, not certainty, but probability, must be the guide of human life. This belief in the unlimited scope and authority of reason was strengthened by the prevailing scientific temper and achieve-ments. The work of Bruno, Copernicus, Galileo, Kepler, and Gassendi, had its counterpart on English soil. In the seventeenth century Francis Bacon had insisted in his *Novum Organum* on the need for precise observation and classification. The founding of the Royal Society in the reign of Charles II brought scientists together in a discussion of pure and applied science. It is true that men like Robert Boyle and Sir Isaac Newton were religiously minded and openly rejected the scepticism of Thomas Hobbes. Nevertheless the researches which led to the discovery of gravitation and of the calcu-lus changed the mode of thinking in eighteenth-century England. A book of that period which won great fame and had large sales was written by Matthew Tindal and entitled *Christianity as Old as Crea-tion* (1730). As the title implies, Tindal argued that natural religion has always existed in its perfection and therefore revelation can add nothing to it. When David Hume wrote his celebrated *Essay on Miracles*, even that favourite line of Christian apologetics seemed to have been destroyed. This sceptical attitude was attacked by writers as different as Henry Dodwell, William Law, and John Wesley, but they were powerless to alter the main current of belief in the sufficiency of man guided by his own unaided reason.

The whole movement gained strength from Continental schools of thought. Important English writers such as Tillotson and Locke could maintain a natural belief in the supernatural, but this seemed an unsatisfactory midway resting-place to French philosophers. They took their stand on a defiant Deism. Voltaire would have nothing to do with Christianity. In his work on Bolingbroke he wrote: 'Every man of sense, every good man, ought to hold the Christian sect in horror.' On the other hand, he argued in his *Dictionnaire Philoso-phique* that getting rid of Jesuits did not involve getting rid of God. The appeal was not to faith, but always to reason. 'To believe in a wise creator', he wrote in his article on Faith, 'is reasonable.' Rous-seau's approach was at once more mystical and more emotional than that of Voltaire but he also had no place for orthodox belief; not for him the sinner's entire need of God's grace. 'My son,' he said, 'keep your spirit always in such a state as to desire that there be a God and you will never doubt it . . . a just heart is the one true temple of God.'

In Germany Leibniz was a contemporary of Sir Isaac Newton, and independently of him discovered the differential calculus. In the tradition of his time, he was not only mathematician, but scientist and philosopher. His *Théodicée* was a sustained argument of great learning designed to show the harmony of faith and reason, and to justify God's ways with men. To philosophers he is known by his theory of monads, all agreeing in a pre-established harmony, so that beneath diversity there is the fundamental unity of creation.

The great Immanuel Kant was early influenced by this dominant Leibniz-Wolffian school of thought. In his later life he developed, in his *Critique of Pure Reason*, his own distinctive philosophy, but he was still concerned with the scope as well as the limits of reason. Reason, he argued, could not deal with *noumena* (things in themselves), but only with phenomena, since the latter do not exist in themselves but only in relation to mind. Even accepting these limitations, Kant argued that reason could vindicate the scientific claims of mathematics and physical knowledge. Though it could not accept or deny the Christian Creeds, reason could still justify the moral life and the validity of the moral order of the universe. The one unqualified good thing is the good will; by this Kant meant the following of no course of action which we cannot will to be universally obeyed. Here certainly was a noble attempt to show that the moral law was a conclusion of reason, and that therefore the rational life must be the moral life. Like other eighteenth-century philosophers, however, Kant's idealism rested on a simplified view of human nature which no theologian could accept.

This belief in man's power to deliver himself by reason was no special preserve of philosophers. It was part of the chatter of the coffee houses; it was accepted by the literary salons of Europe. It was the stock-in-trade of political philosophers. Rationalism had crept into the pulpit, and those who speak of Methodism and the Evangelicals must also speak of Socinianism and its effects on Congregationalists and Presbyterians. When John Wesley made his famous apologia, he addressed it as *An Earnest Appeal to Men of Reason and Religion*.

Edmund Burke differed greatly in his political views from William Godwin or Thomas Paine, and Mirabeau's views were different from Robespierre's. Yet despite the wordy warfare over the course of events in France, attackers and defenders agreed that reason must be used to remove unreasonable and harmful forms of government and to construct a society to serve men's needs. In the words of Professor W. H. McNeill,[1] 'the central idea that government should be a

[1] *Past and Future.*

creature of human contrivance designed to serve human wishes and convenience won general acceptance in most of Western Europe'.

The French Revolution was but one aspect of that tide of human thought which in England was called the Romantic Revival. Walter Pater coined his own phrase in writing of its effects. He said: 'The Renaissance of the fifteenth century was great in what it designed. Much it aspired to do was achieved in the *éclaircissement* of the nineteenth century.' These words are attempts to convey an impression of resurgent man, following a path lighted by his own reason, pulling down and building up his social and political institutions, and always confident of his power to compass his own ends. When Shelley chose Prometheus for an epic he rejected the lame conclusion of Aeschylus. Suffering, sin, and death were passing ills; Prometheus must be unbound. The world was his to conquer; in his aspirings he was the romantic counterpart of Wordsworth's 'Happy Warrior'.

A poet can often be the ears and eyes of his age. He catches the groping feelings of the multitude and puts them into words. The most significant feature of the century's close was not political, not literary, but economic. The Industrial Revolution was beginning to change the face of the world. Science was becoming linked with technology. Modern history had begun. If you would supply man with an adjective, then in this age you must speak of economic man. That is how Adam Smith, Ricardo, and Malthus regarded him, and they were the prophets of their age. Jeremy Bentham took small account of aesthetic pursuits if they left a man unhappy: 'Better a pig satisfied than Socrates dissatisfied.'

To be sure there were voices raised in protest. Thomas Carlyle, Charles Dickens, John Ruskin, and William Morris were only heard above others because of their greater eloquence. Ruskin spoke of a rocky valley between Bakewell and Buxton 'divine as the vale of Tempe, where the gods might be seen morning and evening—Apollo and the sweet Muses of the Light'. But, he went on: 'You enterprised a railroad . . . you blasted its rocks away . . . and now, every fool in Buxton can be at Bakewell in half an hour, and every fool in Bakewell at Buxton.'[2] In an unforgettable phrase he declared 'there is no wealth but life'.[3] Yet strange and powerful as were the voices raised against absorption in material prosperity, the rich continued happily to become richer and the poor suffered the consequences. In Europe, in America, in Australia, and later in South Africa, the prizes were given to the enterprising and thrustful. The social type represented

---

[2] *Praeterita.* Joanna's Cave.   [3] *Unto this Last*, Essay iv.

by the 'gold digger' of today sprang from the gold-digging of yesterday. Those gold rushes in their turn were but local manifestations of
a gold rush which marked the age.

England of course had a fifty years' start in her industrialization.
To keep pace with ever-increasing production she needed ever-increasing markets. We acquired the Empire, said J. R. Seeley, 'in a fit
of absence of mind'. Always trade followed the flag. The splashes of
imperial red on the geography maps grew larger. In Rudyard Kipling
there was even a poet of Empire to give Imperialism a suitable aura:

> *For the Lord our God Most High*
> *He hath made the deep as dry,*
> *He hath smote for us a pathway to the ends of all the earth!*

It was hard for pioneers, whether in the old world, the new world, or
'down-under', to believe they were lost sinners. That might be the
verdict of the Bible, but if so, the Bible was not to be trusted. And so
indeed it seemed when Charles Darwin's *Origin of Species* was published in 1859. To undermine belief in a special act of creation which
lasted six days of a single week seemed to great numbers to undermine
the whole authority of the Bible.

It was a double process. The Bible went, with its view of man's
utter dependence on God, and Evolution stepped into its place, with a
rosy picture of man's upward but rewarding climb to a not-so-distant
peak of achievement. In a sense the Renaissance and the centuries
which succeeded it had prepared him for this moment. The philosophers had told him that he had the necessary reason to accomplish his
aims; the scientists had assured him of the necessary instruments at
his hands; the economists had taught him that John Bunyan was very
wrong to call the world 'a wilderness' (it could be made a very comfortable place with every modern convenience); and biology now
asserted that out of struggle progress would inevitably result. Man
was secure in his universe.

Herbert Spencer was a highly reputable philosopher with a great
vogue in nineteenth-century England. He had no hesitation on the
subject. In his *Social Statics* he declared: 'Progress is not an accident
but a necessity. . . . It is a part of nature.' The poets were ready to
join him. Tennyson's *Locksley Hall* is a set of variations on the theme
of an exciting morrow:

> *Yet I doubt not thro' the ages one increasing purpose runs,*
> *And the thoughts of men are widen'd with the process of the suns.*

Browning was a Christian and Algernon Swinburne an agnostic, but both were equally optimistic.

On the Continent, Henri Bergson spoke of the *élan vital* as the clue to the evolutionary process. In this century two figures of world stature wrote in their different idiom of the ascent of man. In a whole series of scientific romances, philosophical novels and treatises, H. G. Wells popularized the idea of the coming age of splendour made possible by the scientific attitude and its achievements; and George Bernard Shaw hammered home the same idea in such plays as *Back to Methuselah* and *Man and Superman*. In this latter play the whole dialogue in Hell is a sustained argument on the Life Force and its work. It is the struggling god involved in the machine and needing men as its instruments if life is to be thrust forward.

In this pattern of thought, sin had no proper place. In his notable book *The Origin and Propagation of Sin* (1903), F. R. Tennant developed the argument that sin could be explained as a remaining survival of man's animal ancestry. In his long pilgrimage from the jungle to the city of life man has slowly learned to use his impulses and passions rightly. He still suffers from ignorance, superstition, and wilfulness, but with certain setbacks he goes forward to his goal.[4] Behind the teaching on the 'social gospel' lay the belief that if men would overcome social evils, and by certain reforms achieve the social good, they would bring in the new Jerusalem. No wonder Blake's poem of that name was so popular as a song, and no wonder that the verses of John Addington Symonds accorded so well with the spirit of the age:

> *These things shall be! A loftier race*
> *Than e'er the world hath known shall rise,*
> *With flame of freedom in their souls,*
> *And light of knowledge in their eyes.*

Those were the days when the local baritone at the church social sang Henley's 'Invictus' with great effect. The Christian audience warmly applauded the pagan sentiment:

> *I am the master of my fate:*
> *I am the captain of my soul.*

In our own century we have reaped the consequences of what S. R. Hopper in his *Crisis of Faith* has called 'the faithless culture projecting from a faithless mind'. From theology we passed through metaphysics to philosophy, and on to economics, to find answers to our

[4] See also *The Concept of Sin* (1912).

questions about man. It was not through the preaching of the divines but through the hard pressure of events that we realized we had asked the wrong questions and the answers received were irrelevant.

History has been described as offering a long-deferred term for repentance. There may have been a Dr Johannes Faustus of great learning who lived in the sixteenth century and Johann Spies may therefore have had historical foundation for his description of Faust and the compact with the Devil. The point is of no great importance, since the legend of Faust has in some form or other gripped the mind of man as an allegory of human existence. Simon Magus is the New Testament Faust; the Everyman of the Morality Play is the medieval Faust; Peer Gynt is the Scandinavian Faust. In Christopher Marlowe's play, Faustus seeks temporal power. In Goethe's masterpiece he remains unsatisfied with learning, with the satisfaction of bodily appetites, with wealth and with authority; only in the service of men does he know any true joy. The variations are many, but the theme is always the same.

Renaissance man, blown up to twentieth-century proportions, is still Faust. Dependence on God is denied. He has vast learning, ever-increasing riches. He can indulge his passions and his appetites. He can deal with the Devil on equal terms, for all authority has been given him. Yet no Faust either in history or in legend has been happy on such terms. Sooner or later the reckoning must be made. Marlowe's words have a modern ring:

O lente, lente currite noctis equis:
The stars move still, time runs, the clock will strike.

There is no authoritative account of Faust's end. If he persists in folly the Devil may take him; if he repents he may discover his creatureliness and in God's mercy be delivered. It is he who must decide. There is a strange story told in the Acts of the Apostles. Sapphira follows Ananias in an act of treachery to God, and Peter says: 'The feet of those that buried your husband are at the door and they will carry you out.' There is none of this generation with keen hearing who has not heard the scraping of the feet outside the door. They wait to carry us out. But the door need never open.

CHAPTER III

THE SHAME AND GLORY OF MAN

THE phrase belongs to Pascal. He said that man was 'the shame and glory of the universe'. Four hundred years of Renaissance thinking asserted his glory. It is in this present century that we have known his shame. By future writers 1914 will be regarded as a great watershed of history. No one in the early summer of that year could have believed that a shot which killed an Arch-Duke at a place hitherto unknown would cause reverberations throughout the world. An earlier shot had, of course, in some measure had that result; and in the War of American Independence, the crowd gathered round the newly opened Concord Monument sang feelingly the verse of Ralph Waldo Emerson:

> *By the rude bridge that arched the flood,*
> *Their flag to April's breeze unfurled,*
> *Here once the embattled farmers stood,*
> *And fired the shot heard round the world.*

But this time a trigger was pulled and the whole story of mankind was changed. In that fateful August it was realized in brutal fashion that an imposing superstructure is of no avail if foundations are insecure.

Twentieth-century civilization was impressive, but it rested precariously on the character of man. When the foundations gave way, the whole edifice came tumbling to the gound. La Fontaine was right: the swollen frog can never be a bull; if it continues to inflate itself it will not even remain a frog. For four years we went through the hell of modern warfare. Military aircraft and poison gas were used. Men toiled terribly for a few yards of Flanders mud only to lose it once more. The two sides were like gigantic wrestlers locked in each others arms, wearing away each other's life, until suddenly one collapsed, and the other, weary and exhausted, could claim the victory. The true significance was not in the frenzied cheering on 11th November 1918, but the observance of two minutes' silence on each successive year.

Coming out of the first World War was like emerging from a horribly long and dark and frightening tunnel. Men blinked their eyes because they were no longer accustomed to the light of day. The air was still full of slogans. The world was to be made 'safe for democracy'; but already there was the question mark of Russia. England was to be 'a land fit for heroes to live in'; but soon returned soldiers felt fortunate to find a job. Germany was to be 'squeezed until the pips squeaked'; but if that was done, how could she pay her way, receive our imports, and help to restore the normal balance of trade? By the nineteen-twenties even the optimistic were asking awkward questions and a mood of disillusionment made the taste of victory like Dead Sea fruit.

Despite the gallant idealism of President Woodrow Wilson, America turned its back on Europe and returned to its former policy of isolation. The Great Powers persisted in treating the freshly formed League of Nations as a bargaining centre where nations clinging to absolute sovereignty still pursued their own interests without seeking through the League a common policy to their common advantage. An understanding with Germany was bedevilled by the fears and hatred of the French. A like vindictiveness, more generally shared, made impossible a realistic understanding of the economic situation. Germany must 'be bled white', though all suffer in consequence. Delays in demobilization, difficulty in finding work, and the restlessness engendered by war, led to unsettlement and strikes in many countries. Between 1919 and 1920 there were, according to Anthony Weymouth, three thousand trade disputes in England alone. By June 1921 two and a half million were unemployed.

The instinctive reaction was to fly from it all. In Australia, America, and England this was the time to forget. Those who have read F. L. Allen's fascinating account (entitled *Only Yesterday*) of American life in the twenties will remember how the author traces in 'those ballyhoo years' a pattern of licence and excitement which leads inevitably to Chapter 13. That chapter, describing the last year of the decade, is entitled 'The Crash'. London had its 'bright young things, who painted the town red' and so often stole the headlines with their escapades. A sort of Chinese pantomime named 'Chu Chin Chow' had world popularity and enjoyed in London a record run of three years. There was another musical show called 'A Little Bit of Fluff', which was as weighty as its title but enjoyed great success. In the theatre, people were flocking to see the succession of light comedies of Noël Coward.

But the temper of the decade is best illustrated by the success of Aldous Huxley's novels, and the verse and prose of D. H. Lawrence. Both advocated an escape into a sex mysticism in which life could be realized through giving rein to the appetites. 'My great religion', said D. H. Lawrence, 'is a belief in the blood, the flesh, as being wiser than the intellect. We can be wrong in our minds, but what our blood feels is always true.' And even more starkly, in *The White Peacock*, he cried: 'Be a good animal, true to your animal instincts.'

It was in this decade that *vers libre* had its brief flowering. In the hands of an accomplished technician like Ezra Pound, it was subtle and ingenious. Generally, however, it gave an excuse for the lazy to retreat from the discipline of true poetry and to scatter their odd words upon a page in an attempt to deceive the simple. The movement had its vogue because it was born out of a particular mood. When that mood passed, *vers libre* died with few to feel a pang. Also at this time the history of art records the curious phenomenon of surrealism. It was almost as short lived as D. B. Wyndham Lewis's earlier Vorticism and it represented the same flight from reality. As the word implied, the artists sought inspiration in the subconscious world of the mind. Indeed it owed as much to Freud's theories of the deeper levels of consciousness as it did to the contemporary flight from harsh realities. It lingered in a no-man's-land between fact and fantasy. The phase was evanescent. No one has been more severe in his criticism of extremism than Wyndham Lewis himself in his recent book, *The Demon of Progress in the Arts*. For him it is 'a mad bug'. Now he has no time for the 'exhibitionist extremist', but that is because he writes his present Art-criticism in the fifties and not in the twenties.

The mood of disillusionment was induced by the deepening realization that the instruments upon which man had depended for his further advance had broken in his hands. People rush to forget only when there is something unpleasant to remember.

The great pride of twentieth-century man had been the enlarged opportunities in education. When after a series of Acts, education was provided freely by the Government for children up to the age of fourteen years, it was generally believed that an educated people would avoid former follies and establish a new, enlightened, and peaceful order of life. After the first World War the sad truth came home to men that education with a wrong set of ideas had turned a great nation like Germany into a vast military machine that rushed on to its own destruction. It was further realized that education might give a man more knowledge, and more skill in handling that knowledge, but it would not give him the will to use that knowledge in the service of his fellow men. It might only give him greater *expertise* in the pursuits of his own private interests. An educated rogue is more dangerous than an ignorant burglar. Gradually it became recognized that behind education must be vision, character, and a true set of values. Education by itself was not enough.

Similarly the twenties brought a growing realization that science was not a magic talisman. A century that had brought 'wireless' into common speech, and invented the internal-combustion engine, and enabled men to speed through the air and under the water, was apt to suppose that all things could be brought under man's dominion. Poison gases and the increased efficiency of destructive weapons drove deep the bitter understanding that science by itself is neither bad nor good. Everything depends on the use to which it is put. It can be used to construct or to destroy. Science is an abstract term used to denote the work and conclusions of scientists. To lose oneself in the abstract by talking airily of science and its endless possibilities is to forget that all depends on scientists who are but fallible men subject to many outside pressures. If their country demands it, their energies will be devoted to the service of death. Once again, therefore, came the realization that if man's scientific ingenuity was not to encompass his own destruction there must be vision, character, and a true set of values. The solution lay in the realm of the spirit.

This was even true in economics. J. M. Keynes had not yet popularly arrived to break down the rigidity of the economic 'laws'. Understand those laws, work them properly, profit by industrial techniques, and it was thought that prosperity would come. It did not come. Even before the war there was an unemployment problem, but in the twenties the normal figure in England was about two million men out of work. The industrial situation was not greatly different in other parts of the world. Mounting uncertainty and loss of confidence culminated in the Wall Street crash of 1931. Then in every part of the world came the same story of food being lost whilst millions were starving. Wheat was destroyed, coffee was burnt, fish were thrown overboard, cotton was re-ploughed into the ground, and vast numbers lived in primary poverty. The economists had their cliché. We have learnt to produce, they said, but we have not learnt to distribute. Amongst laymen a simpler word was used: we have learnt to produce, they said, but we haven't yet learnt how to share. This was in effect giving a spiritual answer to an economic problem. It showed the realization that if economics was properly to function, there must be vision, character, and a true sense of values.

The world in the twenties had made an important discovery. The instruments men use, such as education, science, and economics, had no independent vitality. Of themselves they were morally neutral. Everything depended upon the use to which they were put. This in turn depended on the users of the instruments. Could men rightfully employ what lay in their hands? Had they the necessary vision, the required strength of character, the acceptance of absolute values? The debate had turned at last on man's soul.

If the nineteen-twenties were the decade of disillusionment; the thirties marked the beginning of two decades of despair. It was not a despair of man's gifts—they were great and various—it was a despair about man himself. The mood had many facets. T. S. Eliot had written *The Waste Land* in 1922 and since then had passed from that cynicism to religious conviction. But it was the earlier Eliot who set his stamp on the young poets writing in the thirties. W. H. Auden, Stephen Spender, Louis Macniece, and Cecil Day Lewis took their text from Eliot's *Hollow Men:*

> *We are the hollow men*
> *We are the stuffed men*
> *Leaning together*
> *Headpiece filled with straw.*

They believed, as he had said, that they were in the 'valley of dying stars', the 'broken jaw of our lost kingdoms'. Accepting his premises, how could they resist his conclusion:

> *This is the way the world ends*
> *Not with a bang but a whimper.*

Some of the poets, in their very despair, looked to Marxist Socialism as a solution, and even sealed their faith by dying on the Republican side in the Spanish Civil War. The mood was by no means confined to England. It was the American poet Archibald Macleish who wrote: 'The conquest of cosmos by science is no lordship. It is finding out how. We do not wish to be kings. We wish to know How. And we know. And we are bored to death. To death.'[1]

Expressionism, which characterized the art forms of the thirties, had its many shades of difference. Wyndham Lewis prophesied for them all a plunging over the side of the precipice 'into a nihilistic nothingness or zero'. He has not asked, with all his questions, the profounder question: Why this mode of expression? In some of the works of artists like Ben Nicholson and Barbara Hepworth, there is, in Herbert Read's words, 'no connexion with the world of appearances'. Such art, he says, 'does not depend for its values on any reference to the external world'. If the artist thus retreats into his own citadel, is not this a gesture of despair?

[1] See S. R. Hopper, *The Crisis of Faith*, p. 50.

Freud was known and widely read in the twenties, but it was in the next decade that his influence was greatest. He popularized the 'unconscious' and made men aware that beneath the thin veneer of civilized man lay the instincts of the wolf and the tiger. It is not the one-ninth of the iceberg above the water which is dangerous to the mariners but the eight-ninths submerged beneath the waves. Similarly, it is in the dark subterranean levels of mind that the danger to corporate life exists. If we ever stretched forward to pick up three words representing a revolution of thought in the modern world, they would be evolution, relativity, and the unconscious. All the prophets object to what their disciples have made of their teaching. Whatever Freud may have desired, those who eagerly swallowed his teaching conjured up a fearsome picture of mankind driven by dark irrational impulses and moved primarily by the instinct of sex. They did not mean by sex what Freud intended; but the notion grew that the hand at the rudder was by no means firm and the ship might easily be lost. In a word, man was not to be respected, but regarded with a compound of pity, puzzlement, and dread. This was an approach to one's species that easily settled into despair.

The sombreness of the prevailing mood was partly caused and partly heightened by the swift march of events. When the ordinary man in the thirties came home from work and finished his evening meal and settled down to read his evening paper, what was the fare provided? It was one long series of words, and every word spoke of war. He read of Manchukuo, Abyssinia, Spain, China, Czecho-Slovakia, and finally Poland. Small wonder that he let his newspaper fall to the ground, looked across at his wife, and said: 'I don't like it.' The ordinary man is the juryman. On his common sense ultimately we all depend. His intuition did not in this case mislead him. We were like the Gadarene Swine. Nothing could stop the momentum of events. We were being hurled headlong over the abyss. We had not long to wait. In September 1939 the babies of the first World War were fighting in the second. The post-Renaissance world had come to its end. The pretensions had been scattered to the winds; the glory of man had become his shame. No longer was he the 'paragon'; rather he had become 'unaccommodated man—a poor bare forked animal'. The wheel had come full circle.

The extent of man's despair was not immediately apparent. In the second World War everyone was involved, and in some places of the conflict those at home endured more of war's hazards than those on military operations. The need for increased production, for constant alertness, for adaptability to the constantly changing pattern of events, induced a certain *élan* of spirit. For multitudes without a name, going a mediocre way from cradle to grave, it was exhilarating to be a participant and not a spectator in the mightiest war of all history. The need for action drove out the melancholy which springs from reflection. Men had no time to indulge in 'nerves'. It is since the war that the crowds wait upon the psychiatrists and the mental homes are full.

In six years of war men passed through the whole gamut of emotion, until victory came with 'all passion spent'. There was an exhaustion of body, but even more, a sheer tiredness of spirit. One side had outstripped the other in men, materials, and technical ingenuity. Weapons of mass destruction had grown steadily more impressive until the grand climax of an Atom Bomb. It was a sorry end, a ragged finish. All the pennons fluttering, and all the bonfires blazing, could not hide the deep disquiet of the human heart. What was this new fury man had unleashed upon his fellow and what consequences would follow in its wake? When the last gun was silent, when the last plane had come to base and the last ship to harbour, the old despair could no longer be held at bay. In the quiet, man had time to look at himself in a mirror. He was profoundly shocked by what he saw. After two thousand years of the Christian Era he had come within measurable distance of destruction. The delicate mechanism of civilization had been so damaged that some wondered whether it was irreparable. The wrong use of gifts that could have brought him into a Promised Land had engulfed him in bitter loss.

It was not surprising that the cult of existentialism rising in France, Germany, Belgium, and Italy, was becoming popular in other countries of Europe as well. There was even a Christian variety, with Gabriel Marcel as its chief exponent; but fundamentally the philosophy was atheistic. Whether the exponent was a playwright like Jean Paul Sartre or a philosopher like Heidegger, the key-notes were the same. The existentialists all spoke in terms of anguish, abandonment, and despair. The word itself had first been used by Kierkegaard. For him it meant the existentialist moment in which the soul encounters God, the brook Jabbok in the life of every fervent seeker; it therefore had a truly Christian connotation. 'Relate yourself', he said, 'absolutely to the Absolute.' But now the Christian Sacrament had become the Black Mass. The post-war existentialists declared that we must relate ourselves absolutely to the relative. According to the temper of their teaching they urged action or reflection, pleasure or pursuit; but always they believed the posturings were on an empty stage, and the back-cloth was of time and not eternity. Shortly after the end of the war there was a cabaret in Berlin which attracted great attention. Girls, dressed in black tights, threw a skull one to another. In the background was the rise and fall of a guillotine. All was done to the mournful roll of drums. It dramatized effectively the prevailing mood of dark despair.

The ordinary people in different countries had not heard of existentialism. Even if they had, they never bothered to try to understand it. Nevertheless, like Molière's M. Jourdain who had been speaking prose without knowing it, they were largely of the same opinion, they shared the same mood. One English paper spoke of the post-war philosophy of 'futilitarianism'—that sense of futility which prompts a man to say: 'Ah, what's the use?' There was a growing disposition to believe that the battle goes to the strong, the race goes to the swift, and the weakest go to the wall. We strive, and struggle, and suffer, and then we are tumbled into the dusty unremembering grave. But if death ends all, and if tomorrow the undertaker may come, then why not eat, drink, and be merry?

It is not always remembered that God and goodness are etymologically joined. The two words go together, and if one is doubted the other will fall into the same discredit. When despair finally seized the soul of man and he saw himself vainly struggling in a meaningless universe, it was easy in losing religion to lose its sanctions. Only the man who believes in God uses the words 'ought' and 'ought not' with any conviction; for the rest the simple reference is to pain and pleasure. When there are no absolute standards, men's conduct is determined by the avoidance of what is painful and the enjoyment of what is pleasant. But when moral considerations no longer arise, the pursuit of one's own pleasure may be at the common expense. These were the years when the divorce rate rose to ever greater heights. It was the period of juvenile delinquency in aggravated form—the age of the 'spiv' and the 'cosh boy'. Crimes of violence, often of murder, began to shock the tired public conscience.

That by itself was a good omen and it was not an isolated one. By the end of the forties the faintly beating heart of Europe had begun to grow stronger. UNRRA had come with its promise of life, and later, Marshall Aid stimulated the process of recovery. There is a stage in exhaustion when the patient is too weak even to ask questions; nothing matters. When the danger-point is passed, and even convalescence is left behind, then the ugly and sinister obtrude unpleasantly on the consciousness. Questions are asked and a fresh assessment of life is possible. At the close of the fifth decade, a world recovering at last from the blood-letting of war was beginning afresh to grapple with the all-important question—What is man?

It might be argued that the number of answers is equal to the number of individuals; but in fact, despite the endless variations, there are only three main answers that can be given. There is pessimism; there is optimism; there is Christian realism. Since the debate still continues, it would be wise to study these three alternatives in turn.

Before the nineteenth century had closed, satisfaction with post-Renaissance man was no longer universal. Even Tennyson had his moments of doubt:

> *Thou madest man, he knows not why,*
> *He thinks he was not made to die;*
> *And thou hast made him: thou art just.*

With his belief in the 'one-increasing purpose', he was still convinced there lived more faith in honest doubt than in half the creeds. This uneasy balance between faith and doubt, hope and uncertainty, was resolved by Thomas Hardy into a steady unyielding despair. The background of his writing was in the 'ancient permanence of the Egdon waste'. In its sombre indifference to the little humans who scampered over its surface, it was a fitting symbol of the vast unheeding universe in which the drama of life must be played. Tess of the D'Urbervilles is no wanton. She is but a puppet in the hands of the President of the Immortals, and who is he but an 'Aeschylean phrase'? Life has no meaning and therefore no direction. It is in his poetry, and supremely in *The Dynasts*, that he surveys the human scene in vain for One who cares.

> *Like a knitter drowsed,*
> *Whose fingers play in skilled unmindfulness,*
> *The Will has woven with an absent heed*
> *Since life first was; and ever so will weave.*

William Ernest Henley was a popular poet of his day, who had no God, and therefore could only resort to a desperate stoicism.

> *A poor old tramp explains his poor old ulcers.*
> *Life is (I think) a blunder and a shame.*[2]
>   [2] *In Hospital.*

That note of despair was a major note in poetry until the outbreak of the second World War.

This tragic theme of many poets was far more vividly illustrated by the writings of three prophets of world stature—Kierkegaard, Dostoevsky, and Nietzsche. All felt intensely the burden of the world's distress; all knew the intolerable tension between faith and doubt. Two emerged triumphant, like Jacob from his lonely wrestling; they knew the heavenly adversary even though they 'halted on their thigh'—so great a struggle for ever left its mark. Nietzsche had no such deliverance; no God appeared from the night of his struggling. Without the supernatural man must himself become the superman. But this was no cause for laughter. He gave a new content to the phrase 'the death of God': 'Since there ceased to be a God, loneliness has become intolerable: the man who overtops the rest must set to work.' No one fully understands the philosophy of Nietzsche who does not appreciate the pessimism which underlay his strenuous call to action.

Perhaps it is in other quarters, however, that one can best discern the accent of despair. From Europe the great psychologist, C. G. Jung, wrote in his *Modern Man in Search of a Soul:* 'Modern man is the end product of an age-old development, but he is also the worst conceivable disappointment of the hopes of human kind.' He went on to argue that man was aware of this. He had come to know how beneficent were science, technology, and civilization, but also how catastrophic they could be. Today, he asserted, there is 'the same optimism, the same organization, the same political aspirations, the same phrases and catch-words at work. How can we but fear that they will inevitably lead to further catastrophes?' Written six years before the outbreak of the second World War, his grim discussion of the 'spiritual problem of modern man' was strikingly prophetic.

From America in that same period, Walter Lippmann gave the world his *Preface to Morals.* He spoke in chapter headings of the problem of unbelief in which 'Whirl is King; the loss of certainty; the acids of modernity; the breakdown of authority; and the lost provinces.' Many found the first part of the book, in its relentless probing of contemporary ills, more searching than its conclusion.

From England H. G. Wells wrote books that were despairing both in analysis and in their final summary. There is no pessimism like that of an optimist turned sour. The man who wrote of the shape of things to come had a nightmarish notion of its form in the last few years of his life. In his *Fate of Homo Sapiens* and *Mind at the End of its Tether*, he conveyed a philosophy in a title. Man would in the end destroy himself and the world would be dominated by monstrous reptiles; the animal orders of creation would be reversed; man's story would be that told by an idiot.

The theological parallel to this despair was in Barthianism, a school of religious thought which often went to greater extremes than was merited by the writings of Karl Barth himself. The stress on God at the expense of man led to the criticism that man decreased that God might increase. Certainly Barth's commentary on Romans was a theological landmark. In it he declared that 'man is his own lord, his creatureliness is his chain. His sin is his debt. His death is his fate. His world is a formless ebbing and retreating chaos of natural psychical and other powers. His life is an appearance.' Titanism means for Barth the failure of modern man to know his creatureliness, and therefore to know his utter and complete dependence on God. God is transcendent in His majesty and power. He is the Absolute, the entirely Other, the '*Deus absconditus*' of Martin Luther. In His infinite unconditioned qualitative difference God stands against us, and for His Word we wait. There is no two-way traffic. Man cannot find a way to God; God must choose His own way to men. In a phrase he often used, Barth declared that God must come even as the vertical line strikes down to the horizontal. Revelation therefore becomes all-important; the word is only known in the Word made flesh. Even so it is not the human Jesus, who remains for Barth 'The great Incognito'; but the divine risen Christ attested by apostolic preaching, who speaks the everlasting 'Yea' of God. Barth himself has modified Barth, but it was the earlier Barth who so profoundly affected theological thinking between the two wars. How little room it left for political reconstruction and social reform, and how greatly it hammered home the plight of man! Barth would put his own special emphasis on a saying of Jesus about demons: 'This kind', he said, 'goeth not forth save by prayer and fasting.' Other writers of world stature such as Aulén, Reinhold Niebuhr, Berdyaev, and Brunner, were kinder to man and his aspirations, but substantially they left the same picture of man's littleness and the towering greatness of God.

In direct contrast with this pessimism about man there still survived the liberal optimistic Utopianism of the humanists. Humanism is a word with many shades of meaning. There are classical humanists like the late G. Lowes Dickinson, Gilbert Murray, and Richard Livingstone, who retain their faith in the values of Greek culture and their relevance for the world of today. There are political humanists, notably the Marxians, who believe that in the rearrangement of society man can achieve his age-long aspirations. There are the scientific humanists who believe that in accepting the scientific spirit and adopting the scientific attitude man can find his way to a stream-lined chromium-plated antiseptic Utopia. Finally, there are humanists who reject any adjectival qualifications, but simply accept the fact that man is the measure of all things and therefore the sole architect of his own destiny.

Until the outbreak of the first World War all humanists breathed a congenial air. They were the true interpreters of the contemporary mood. Then came the deluge. Still their optimism persisted. Neither wars nor rumours of wars could break this spirit. Speak of lust, treachery, cruelty, and they could also speak of 'the invincible spirit of man'. They might and did regret the stimulus to man's worst instincts, but they could rhapsodize over his courage and hope, and his limitless determination to go forward. Always they could refer to the technical achievements of man; put your hand into such a bag and you could pick out marvels as various as the Mersey Tunnel, the Tennessee Valley Authority, the Sydney Bridge, Radar, and Television. But of course a recital like that was meaningless, because it could have no end. Why not, for example, turn to another field and speak of insulin, radium, and penicillin? Of if your fancy chose, why not dwell on man's heroism and think of Polar expeditions, or a mile run in four minutes, or the ascent of Everest?

When the second World War was over, the demise of humanism was announced in many a good sermon. But no undertaker could find the corpse. It reminds one of Gracie Fields's song of an obstinate old gentleman: 'He's dead but he won't lie down.' Unabashed humanists such as J. B. S. Haldane, Julian Huxley, Lancelot Hogben, and C. H. Waddington, had still a large world-following. From the Arctic Circle to the Antipodes, great numbers of 'activists' were cheerfully agreeing with Joseph Needham, the eminent biologist, that 'history is on our side'. The scientific camp amongst the humanists was unabashed by a half-century of violence. They asserted that a scientific attitude to life, sustained by the scientific spirit, could deliver us from our doldrums and land us on the sun-lit heights. This optimism is still reflected in the popular Press. There is an enormous demand for science fiction, and within that *genre*, for 'space fiction'. 'Flying saucers' lend a certain credence to the idea of beings on other planets, superior to ourselves and therefore challenging us to ever greater endeavour. It is a mark of many books and weekly papers read by boys and girls that there should be a hero who is larger than life. It is not only that he is unbelievably brave, resourceful, and masterful, but that he has all the resources of modern science to aid him. Sometimes, indeed, in his power to transport himself vast distances within the split second, or in his proof against all possible attack, there is a deliberate flight into the realm of magic; but it is the magic of the Superman who needs no God to help him.

Here then are two contradicting twentieth-century assumptions about man. One is pessimistic because it remembers his shame; the other is optimistic because it remembers his glory. Neither position is satisfactory, and he is a witless wight who supposes he must choose between them. To be pessimistic about man is to have a sterile philosophy. Out of such barrenness nothing fruitful can come; it leaves one with the necessity for existence without a dynamic for living. On the other hand, humanism in any form is condemned on two counts: it does not take account of the facts of history nor of the facts of human nature. A century which has known poison-gas and atomic bombs; Belsen, Dachau, and the Polish gas-chambers, mass liquidations and brain-washing, is no period for sentimentalizing over man and his achievements. It leaves one with the picture of the clever child in the nursery who can construct his elaborate working model, and then with a clumsy sweep of the hand, knock it down to the floor.

Nor is this all. Behind this sorry story of man's success and failure, his capacity to invent and then to destroy, lies the riddle of human nature. The humanistic diagnosis is too naïve and over-simplified to do justice to the complexity of man's spirit. It finds what it is looking for, and averts its gaze from what it does not like. It cherishes the romantic illusion of Renaissance thinking about man, despite the piled-up incontrovertible evidence of his clay feet. In a word, it does not fit the facts.

Truth is often to be found midway between two extremes. We need neither the pessimists nor optimists. The times demand a Christian realism. The day is far past when we need to go back to Genesis to justify a belief in the fallen nature of man. The origin of sin is still a nice point of dispute among theologians, but the fact of his sinfulness is not to be denied. One need go no farther than the morning paper or the radio bulletin. In the screaming headlines of the world's daily news is ample evidence both of man's shame and man's glory. One item will record a savage murder and the next a deed of breath-taking heroism; it is still a record of the same human nature—

not Prospero or Caliban, but Prospero and Caliban. There is a depth
of insight in the doctrine of original sin not given to humanistic
probings. But we must set the mind free from the frame-work of
allegory and recognize that it implies also an original virtue.

Man was made in the image of God. God breathed into man and he
became a living soul. Christian thinking begins there. It affirms the
imago Dei even in the worst of man. 'The spirit of man is the candle
of the Lord.' Because of that he can know both ecstasy and remorse.
He had a divine beginning and has an immortal destiny. Of Toussaint
L'Overture, Wordsworth said:

> *Thy friends are exultations, agonies,*
> *And love, and man's unconquerable mind.*

It is a commentary on the grandeur and dignity of man. The
Christian would outsoar any humanist in describing man's inheritance
and his goal. He outstrips him even in speaking of man's present
worth, for he is astonished not only by his mental range but by the
qualities of his spirit. It is in his love, his pity, and compassion, that
he best reveals his Maker's stamp.

But if man can rise into the heavens and move easily among the
stars, he can sink beneath the level of brutes. Always there is the
divided nature and therefore the unending tug of war. In no passage
of literature is it more eloquently described than in the seventh chapter of Paul's letter to the Romans. 'The good which I would I do not:
but the evil which I would not, that I practise . . . O wretched man
that I am! who shall deliver me out of the body of this death?' The
truth of that outburst is written small in the individual heart, and
written large in the pages of history. We are not the measure of all
things. We cannot unaided deliver ourselves. As the modern idiom
puts it: we cannot raise ourselves by our own shoelaces. There is a
contradiction in man which is not to be resolved by the abracadabra
of the scientist, teacher, or reformer. Everyone knows William Blake's
lines in 'The Divine Image':

> *For Mercy has a human heart,*
> *Pity a human face,*
> *And Love, the human form divine,*
> *And Peace, the human dress.*

Not so many remember the poem added by Blake to *Songs of Inno-
cence and of Experience* which lights up the complementary truth:

Cruelty has a Human Heart,
And Jealousy a Human Face;
Terror the Human Form Divine,
And Secrecy the Human Dress.

Both verses are needed if the complex nature of man is to be understood.

What can cope with human sin and who can deal with the sinner himself? Christian theology asserts that only grace can deal with sin, and only a Saviour can help the sinner. The facts of human nature made plain in modern history are driving us to a theology of grace. In its appreciation of the greatness and littleness of man there is no room for either pessimism or optimism. There is instead the recognition that we cannot stand alone. Left to ourselves, we can by our very cleverness encompass our own destruction. As Niebuhr would say, increasing cosmos brings the possibility of increasing chaos. The higher one climbs, the greater the fall. It is the secular prophets who are warning us most loudly of impending doom. They have not hesitated to speak of genocide, and no Old Testament prophet has rivalled them in their pictures of the ultimate horror we are preparing for ourselves. Their one weakness is that it is of little use merely to utter cries of warning or appeals to common sense in a situation so fraught with peril. More, much more, is needed.

The overwhelming need is to recognize our dilemma and the true nature of our deliverance. The call is not just to avoid catastrophe, but to enter into our inheritance. The answer is still in the Gospel of good news. In his shame and glory, man can be remade by God alone. Here is the one true source of forgiveness, deliverance, and renewal: in our weakness, His strength; in our perplexity, His guidance; in our sinfulness, His grace. God and man are workers together, but the sufficiency is of God.

Section II

THE DEBATE ON THE STATE

CHAPTER IV

MORRISON'S PILL

IN his *Past and Present*, Thomas Carlyle complained that he had 'no Morrison's Pill for curing the maladies of Society'. That marvellous Pill has still to be discovered and meanwhile men slowly learn from trial and error as the centuries go by. With the Renaissance came an end to the solidarity of the Middle Ages. The feudal order slowly gave way to nationalism. Even in smaller states the Princes faced each other with a proper sense of pride and independence. They did not lack an apologist. Machiavelli had a fierce dislike of a medieval society based on the sanctions of religion and postulating that government must conserve the spiritual ends of man; he would have none of it. He separated the art of government from morality and regarded religion only as an instrument of government. In his political treatise, *Il Principe* (*The Prince*), he argued that the success of the Prince would depend upon his combining the qualities of the lion and the fox. He must have absolute power and use it without scruple. His own good is the true good of his State.

That was strong meat for English stomachs and it was left to Thomas Hobbes in the seventeenth century to defend the absolutism of the Stuarts. He did not seek to justify the 'divine right of Kings', because he was ready to give an ingenious (and quite indefensible) twist to the theory of an Original Contract.

Machiavelli had thought of men as a pack of wolves (*Homo homini lupus*), and Hobbes took hold of the same idea. In a state of nature, he claimed, there were no arts, no letters and no society, and the life of man was 'solitary, poor, nasty, brutish, and short'.[1] The only deliverance from this fearful state was the contract 'to confer all power and strength upon one man or upon one assembly of men that may reduce all their wills, by plurality of voices, unto one will'. The keeping of order depended therefore upon the complete authority of the Sovereign or the Sovereign body. The nation was unified in 'the unity of the representer'.

This unqualified approval of Sovereign power did not accord with the mood of a nation which had passed through the 'Glorious Revolution' of 1688. In the eighteenth century, Hobbes was discredited and the contract theory returned to its more usual form. This was the age of constitutional monarchy and an appropriate political philosophy

[1] *Leviathan*, Ch. 13.

was demanded. It was supplied in Locke's treatise on *Civil Government*. It is worth remarking that in this century writers in France, America, and England agreed in their conception of the State of Nature. They believed that men originally were simple, innocent, and free from care. This incidentally is what gives particular force to John Wesley's *Thoughts on Slavery*. He is able to emphasize the horrors of the middle passage across the Atlantic and the human misery of the Slave Market tearing members of the same family from one another, because he drew an idyllic picture of Africans in their original habitat. Until there came the cruel whips and irons of the slave traders, they were peaceful and happy and unspoilt.

Accepting, as eighteenth-century philosophers did, this picture of man's early paradisal bliss, it was easy to see how the 'contract' could be made an instrument of bargaining. Locke interpreted a prevailing sentiment in arguing that the agreement to surrender certain powers brought in return certain privileges. Since the authority of the ruler depends on the consent and agreement of the people, their natural rights must be guaranteed. These can be gathered up under the headings of life, liberty, and property. The teaching of Locke was appreciated by Bossuet, Fénelon, and Voltaire. Montesquieu in his *L'Esprit des Lois* was greatly influenced by Locke's insistence that private property is essential to true living, and that its upholding must be a primary aim of government. Thomas Jefferson was the principal architect of the Declaration of Independence (4th July 1776), and more fully than he realized, he was an apt pupil of John Locke. The majestic words of the Declaration are almost a poetic transcription of the somewhat uninspired prose of the English philosopher. 'We hold these truths to be self-evident, that all men are created equal, that they are endowed by their Creator with certain unalienable Rights, that among these are Life, Liberty, and the pursuit of Happiness. That to secure these rights Governments are instituted among Men, deriving their just powers from the consent of the governed. That whenever any Form of Government becomes destructive of these ends, it is the Right of the People to alter or abolish it, and to institute a new Government, laying its foundations on such principles, and organizing its powers in such form, as to them shall seem most likely to effect their Safety and Happiness.'

These words seem an echo of the thought in *Civil Government*. Nor would Locke have quarrelled with the assertion that ultimately the people have the right to rebel. In England, France, and America, the eighteenth century had certain common thought-forms. These included the idea of a happy state of nature, a contract into society by the consent of the majority, the State guarantee of natural human rights, and the final validity of revolt if the State wholly failed in its duty to its members. The drift of Locke's thinking was plainly towards democracy. If government is by consent, if rebellion in the last resort is permissible, and if the rights of the individual are emphasized, then the bias of political thinking is to stress the part and not the whole, the person and not the State. This was not true in the case of Rousseau. He thought of the State in organic terms. The sovereign power is the people gathered in a moral unity and expressing itself in 'the General Will'. Rousseau was never quite sure what ought to be the effective legislative organ. He hovered between the heaven-sent legislator, such as Lycurgus or Calvin, and an assembly of all the people. Neither of these expedients was practicable. It was in his picture of man as the friendly social animal, and of the State as a collective body whose inner cohesion depends on brotherliness, that Rousseau influenced political thinking. There is an echo in the lines of Burns:

> *The social friendly, honest man,*
> *Whate'er he be,*
> *'Tis he fulfils great Nature's plan,*
> *And none but he!*[2]

In the three-part slogan of the French Revolution, it was Rousseau who so largely made liberty and equality come to a climax in fraternity. The crowds who seized on some of his aphorisms to pull down the ancient régime, selected that aspect of his philosophy most suited to their immediate needs. 'Man was born free but is everywhere in chains' made an excellent rallying cry. Rousseau's cloth in fact was cut according to the requirements of the Parisian coat. The profounder teaching on the nature of the State could only be appreciated half a century later.

For at the end of the eighteenth century the air was resonant with demands for the ordinary man. His natural rights must be guaranteed and his freedom secured. The man in the crowd had come into his own. In that sense minor philosophers such as Price, Priestley, Godwin, and Paine, were truly representative of their age. In his *Political Justice*, Godwin was so careful to preserve the untrammelled freedom of the individual that he reduced the functions of government to a minimum. 'Government can have no more than two pur-

[2] *Second Epistle to John Lapraik.*

poses: the suppression of injustice in the community, and its defence against foreign invasion.' The two parts of Tom Paine's *Rights of Man* were in answer to Burke's *Reflections on the French Revolution* and his *Appeal from the New to the Old Whigs*. Nevertheless his style was so lucid and vigorous, and the contents so palatable to so many, that the book stands as the most representative example of the Franco-American school of thinking on the individual and his claims on the State. In England the same goal was reached, but along the road, the political philosophers were joined by the economists. England was at the beginning of its Industrial Revolution and *homo oeconomicus* was taking shape. This 'economic man' had certain recognizable traits. It was assumed that he consulted only his own interests. He bought in the cheapest and sold in the dearest market. These economic axioms came to be accepted as natural laws. Consequently it followed that a man best served the general good by following his own private good.

Adam Smith had no doubt that if the people were set free from Government restriction, and each man, in competition with another, could strive for his own ends, both individual and State would benefit. In his *Wealth of Nations* (1776), he had applied this principle to commerce and urged the adoption of free trade as in the best interests of all. J. B. Hammond declared in his book *The Bleak Age* that 'the freedom to make the most of yourself in competition with your fellow men seemed to the Englishmen of the age the most important of all the personal rights that the French and American Revolutions had proclaimed and vindicated'.

Ricardo is best remembered as an economist for his theory of value, and out of that, his treatment of rents, profits, and wages. But Ricardo was a disciple of Adam Smith and in his *Principles of Political Economy and Taxation* (1817), he developed a system of economics based on the worthwhileness of active competition. It was this conception which dominated the 'Manchester School' of economics and during the first half of the nineteenth century it reigned without a serious rival.

In England, Individualism won its notable triumph during the first half of the nineteenth century, not through philosophers and economists only, but even more because it was carried into the sphere of legislation. This was effected mainly through the genius of Jeremy Bentham whom Brougham described as 'the first legal philosopher that had appeared in the world'. He was guided by the utilitarian principle that the proper end of every law lies in promoting the greatest happiness of the greatest number. He further believed that since every person is usually the best judge of his own happiness, legislation should endeavour to remove all unnecessary restrictions on the free action of an individual. It is these principles which are the basis of John Stuart Mill's noble treatise *On Liberty*. The Benthamite denunciation of needless State interference with individual activity was not an easy tolerance with society as it existed. The great jurist, A. V. Dicey, in his *Law and Opinion in England*, described *laissez-faire* as a war cry. In outlining the trend of Benthamite legislation, he argued that it meant the transference of political power to the middle classes, humanitarian reform of law, the extension of individual liberty, and the adequate protection of rights. The benefits were so notable that they could even agitate Metternich's Europe and be hailed approvingly by the pioneers advancing the frontiers in the new world.

Why then was there such a reversal of opinion that, since the mid-nineteenth century, we have lived (to use Dicey's phrase) in 'an age of collectivism'? The change of mental climate is now so world-wide that it is worth considering what factors operated in England to shape such a revolution.

First came the cry of protest from many quarters against the glaring weakness of individualism. In theory it sounds democratic to set men free to run the common race of life. In practice, however, it disregards the fact that men are not equal and that a race under such conditions imposes a grievous handicap on many. How could the poor compete with the rich, the workmen with the master, the physically disabled with the healthy and vigorous? The series of Select parliamentary committees inquiring into the condition of child and female industrial labour, the treatment of the insane, and the working of the Poor Law, brought to light in the thirties, conditions so shocking that the sensitive were revolted. The Tory philanthropists, Oastler, Fielden, Sadler, and Shaftesbury, were at one in their attack on the conditions and hours in factories. Richard Oastler's *Slavery in Yorkshire* directed attention, not to slaves in the West Indies, but the children in Yorkshire factories. In a letter to the *Leeds Mercury* (1830), he declared that 'thousands of our fellow creatures, the inhabitants of a Yorkshire town, are at this very moment existing in a state of slavery more horrid than are the victims of that hellish slavery—colonial slavery'. Another important protest against *laissez-faire* came from Edwin Chadwick. With his keen nose he smelt the bad drains of England and his reports on the *Sanitary Conditions of the Labour-*

ing Population (1842) and *The Health of Towns* (1844) led to the Public Health Act of 1848 and the beginnings of modern sanitary legislation.

Adding their voices to the growing protest against a complacent individualism came the writers. In his *Latter Day Pamphlets*, Thomas Carlyle attacked unsparingly the injustices perpetuated on the unprivileged by a *laissez-faire* policy of government. Mrs Gaskell in her novel *Mary Barton* not only treated sympathetically the action of workmen in conducting a strike, but she revealed some of the abominable conditions in which the poor lived. 'They began to penetrate the thick darkness of the place only to see there three or four little children rolling on the damp, nay wet, brick floor, through which the stagnant filthy moisture of the street oozed up.' Charles Dickens may not have been a systematic thinker, but none in his century did more to rouse the public conscience to social evils. He did this by his own sensitive observation and by his biting irony. In *Little Dorrit* and in *Bleak House* he inveighed against delay and inefficiency in government and in the Judicature, but in *Hard Times* he smote the principles and consequences of individualism hip and thigh. In Charles Kingsley's novel *Alton Locke* and in the writings of the Christian Socialists generally, there is not only an attack on the old order, but a foreshadowing of the new.

There was a second main reason for the decline of individualism in the mid-century. Generous spirits might attack the results of Benthamite individualism; but why had it arisen at all? In England and on the Continent, socialists arose to question the very premises of the dominant political philosophy. Robert Owen, William Thompson, and Thomas Hodgskin were all convinced that a new approach to education, a new combination of labour forces, a new social reorganization of the State, were all demanded. The Continental socialists went farther. They too wanted a radical re-casting of industry and society, because for them the term 'individual man' had no particular significance. Man was only himself as a member of society and only of worth as a worthwhile member of the State. They dismissed the whole framework of Nature, contracts, and natural rights. If man was but part of the fertile spawn of nature, what essential rights did he possess in himself? In isolation he possessed no rights. The eighteenth-century justification could not even be dismissed as allegory, containing truth. It was fiction containing falsehood. Marx and Engels in their *Communist Manifesto* (1848) used new and vigorous language because their thought-forms were new. The old talk of the individual was replaced by a new appeal to the worker. The rights of man in a hypothetical past were exchanged for a call so to revolutionize society that he would enter into his proper inheritance in a foreseeable future.

A third and last major reason for the decline of individualism in English politics was the changed outlook of the working classes. Chartism was the greatest mass movement of the workers in the first half of the nineteenth century. Julius West in his history of the movement described it as 'a state of mind'. It was a way of thinking which went back to 1780, when a committee of the Westminster electors had drawn up a scheme of constitutional reform which anticipated almost every demand of the Chartists. The full Chartist claim was universal suffrage, payment of members, ballot vote, abolition of property qualifications, annual Parliaments, and equal electoral districts. The People's Charter then summed up the political objectives of reformers for half a century. It was wholly Benthamite in tone. Nothing was expected from Governmental interference. The sole demands were for electoral reform so that every man could exercise his vote. The Chartists refused to ally themselves with Ashley (Shaftesbury), Oastler, Sadler, and Fielden in their campaign for industrial reform. They would not even support Cobden and Bright in their agitation against the repressive Corn Laws. They called the Anti-Corn Law League a 'plague' and often broke up its meetings. They were in fact individualists whose hope lay in a reform of Parliament.

The collapse of Chartism in 1848 changed the direction of working-class aspirations. The shadow of working-class discontent had already helped to accelerate the passage of the Factory and Mine Acts, and the Public Health Act of 1848. Disillusioned and more moderate working-class leadership now turned afresh to Trade Unionism, inspired the growth of Co-operative Societies, and, becoming the left wing of the Liberal party, eventually found a separate existence again in the Labour Party. When old animosities had died, when the salutary effects of the repeal of the Corn Laws and of Peel's finances were recognized, when Palmerston had died and Gladstone's Reform Bill (1866) had been taken up and passed in Disraeli's Government of the next year, an alliance between the middle and working classes was made possible. All householders were enfranchised and the number of voters was almost doubled. Since then, all the Chartist proposals, with the exception of annual Parliaments, have passed into law.

In the very year when Chartism as a movement had disintegrated, the Christian Socialists, by their writings and co-operative schemes, began to come into public notice. The *Tracts of Christian Socialism* (1850) tolled the departing of Benthamite individualism and looked forward to a new era of constructive social legislation.

The story of individualism in Government is not peculiar to this country. Making necessary allowances, the same story with a slower *dénouement* was repeated in certain European countries, in Canada, the United States, and the Antipodes. In all these countries the same fundamental weaknesses were in time discovered. In countries as large as Australia, Canada, and the United States, the process has been protracted because the vigour, initiative and enterprise of the individual have been essential to the opening-up of the country. Without the pioneering spirit, impatient of restrictions and eager to seize opportunities, the countries could not have been developed. In any case there has been, in such vast areas, a ready and always expanding market for the internal consumption of goods. Any form of collectivist interference has therefore seemed to many a strait-jacketing of private enterprise. Even so, the objections raised in England have been raised later in other parts of the world. It has been generally recognized that individualism as a dominant political philosophy leaves the weak, the ignorant, the unprivileged and those handicapped by sickness or age, at a grievous disadvantage. Further, it has been admitted that the assertion of individual rights without adequate reference to the claims of the whole has neither historical nor political justification. Pushed to an extreme, it leads to anarchy. An atomistic democracy lacks any principles of cohesion. A State which is only an aggregation of individuals has no true basis for social living. If every householder digs an artesian well in his garden, it is still not so effective as a municipal water supply.

Thirdly, an individualistic democracy lacks the proper instruments for social, political, and economic reform. The disillusionment of the Chartists is sooner or later shared by all who conceive too narrowly the function of government. Self help is important, but State help is also essential. There must be collectivist legislation if there is to be public service for the private citizen. If the individual were a virtuous, idealistic, uncomplicated human being, individualism might work tolerably well. But if the individual is a divided creature often seeking his private interest and advantage, then political individualism can mean legalized selfishness. In such a society the lack of restriction unduly benefits the powerful and wealthy at the expense of the community. At the World Assembly of Christian Churches in Amsterdam, an unregulated Capitalism was condemned in the same unsparing terms as Communism. The lesson learnt by England in the mid-nineteenth century is now most widely shared. As a political philosophy individualism is not enough.

CHAPTER V

THE WELFARE STATE AND ITS LIMITS

WHEN A. V. Dicey coined the word 'collectivism' to describe the dominant school of political thought since the mid-nineteenth century, he had England alone in his mind. Nevertheless in Canada and the United States, in Scandinavia, in Australia and New Zealand, in France and Germany and Italy, the same process has been in varying degrees at work. It has certain main characteristics. Fundamentally there is the assumption that State intervention is of benefit to the individual. What an individual cannot do so well for himself the State must do for him. The belief is expressed legislatively in various forms of protection for the individual. In many countries there are Workmen's Compensation Acts and restrictions on hours in factory and business undertakings. There are regulations about the condition of labour and the suitable provision for those employed. Certain Acts deal with the essential minimum sanitary requirements in the production and sale of food and drugs. Indeed Public Health Acts, which in England started in 1848, have expanded into the whole sanitary code for the preservation of public health. Another field of collectivist legislation is in securing for all citizens the same opportunities to lead a full life. Long before the Welfare State was conceived, many countries took education out of private hands and made it largely a public concern. The municipal trading which in England became known as 'gas and water socialism' has its counterparts elsewhere. It can be summed up in the satirical comment of Sidney Webb (*Socialism in England*): 'The individualist town councillor will walk along the municipal pavement, lit by municipal gas, and cleaned by municipal brooms, with municipal water, and seeing by the municipal clock in the municipal market that he is too early to meet his children coming from the municipal school, hard by the county lunatic asylum and municipal hospital, will use the national telegraph system to tell them to come by the municipal tramway to meet him in the municipal reading-room, by the municipal art gallery, museum and library, where he intends to consult some national publications in order to prepare his next speech in the municipal Town Hall in favour of the nationalization of canals and the increase of Government control over the railway system. "Socialism, Sir!", he will say, "Don't waste the time of a practical man by your fantastic absurdities. Self help, Sir, individual self help, that's what made our city what it is." '

In this present century, collectivism on a wide front has won resounding victories. It has introduced us to the concept of a planned society, and now, willynilly, we are all members of the Welfare State. It is important to realize that this is not the single-handed achievement of professed socialists. In America, where there is still so much pride in 'rugged individualism' and so much fear of 'red socialism', welfare legislation, whether State or Federal, readily stands comparison with countries of different traditions. In 1935 the passage of the Social Security Act provided for unemployment insurance and old-age pensions; the Tennessee Valley Authority Scheme (TVA), the Works Progress Administration (WPA) and the Civilian Conservation Corps (CCC) are a few of the publicly directed undertakings which spell collectivism in the largest letters. In France, Germany, and Italy, family allowances were introduced earlier and on a more generous scale than in Great Britain. In the early years of this century, W. P. Reeves, in a study of *State Experiments in Australia and New Zealand*, described a course of collectivist legislation which foreshadowed the Welfare State. The Scandinavian countries have initiated a series of welfare measures which in their far-reaching significance amount to a social revolution.

Particular mention ought to be made of Denmark, where the free national system of education covers the middle-aged and elderly as well as the young.

In England itself, the achievement of a planned society was due to all three political parties. The beginnings were all in the golden period of nineteenth-century liberalism. The Old Age Pensions Act (1908) was followed by the National Insurance Act of 1911. After the financial provision for old-age pensioners, came schemes with a much wider area of reference. People between the ages of sixteen and seventy were insured against ill-health and against the incidence of unemployment. Before 1908 the question of insurance was purely personal. In the words of one eminent jurist, such questions 'no more concerned the State than the question whether an individual should wear a black coat or a brown coat'. With the passing of these Acts, the State assumed a greater political legislative and judicial responsibility. The concession of the right to work carried other implications, and the State could hardly stop once it had committed itself to that stretch of road.

During the long period of Tory ascendancy a series of socialistic measures became law. The black period was in the thirties when the national insurance fund broke down under the giant waves of unemployment. There was no attempt to provide either fair maintenance or full employment. Instead, the newly formed Unemployment Assistance Board gave relief which was properly characterized as 'dole'. As Arthur Hugh Clough had said:

Thou shall not kill; but need'st not strive
Officiously to keep alive.[1]

The wider ends of Government were described by Sir William (now Lord) Beveridge in his famous *Report on Social Insurance* (1942). 'There are some who will say that the pursuit of security as defined in the Report, that is to say, income security, is a wholly inadequate aim. That view is not merely admitted but asserted by me. The Plan for Social Security is put forward as part of a general programme of social policy. It is one part only of a general attack on five giant evils: upon the physical Want with which it is directly concerned, upon the Disease which often causes Want and brings many other troubles in its train, upon Ignorance which no Democracy can afford among its citizens, upon the Squalor which arises mainly through haphazard distribution of industry and population, and upon the Idleness which corrupts men and destroys wealth.'

It is this Report of a Liberal which has justly influenced both the Conservative and the Labour parties in formulating a State policy of social welfare. Incidentally, Gladstone would hardly have known it as a Liberal document. The programme involved security of income, State policy for national health, wider governmental provision for education, State financial support for housing, and the redistribution of industry; finally, it adumbrated a policy of full employment. This was the honourable radical tradition of concern for the individual, but also a social philosophy resting on a collectivist basis. Samuel Smiles with his *Self Help* was decently interred. The State must now secure individuals 'from those hazards of personal fortune over which individuals have little or no control'.[2]

The war-time coalition Government was divided in mind over the proposals, and when after much delay its own White Paper was published in 1944, the recommendations were modified. Nevertheless the substance of the scheme was accepted, and when the Labour Party came into power in 1945 the Welfare State had emerged. Apart from Beveridge, the architect of the new order was J. M. Keynes. He

[1] *The Latest Decalogue.*   [2] *Report on Social Insurance.*

showed that a full employment policy was not only right but practicable. The same conclusion was reached by Beveridge in his book *Full Employment in a Free Society* (1944). The vision and administrative capacity of Beveridge, and the brilliance of Keynesian economics, were a powerful stimulus to political and social thinking in free countries throughout the world. Before 1939 the acid test for any social policy was whether 'the State could afford it'. Now the sole question asked was the degree of need. The principle of the Beveridge Plan had been accepted. 'Abolition of want requires . . . adjustment of incomes, in periods of earning as well as interruption of earning, to needs. . . . The plan is based on a diagnosis of want.'

The adoption of the essential principles of the Welfare State in Europe, North America, Australia, and New Zealand means that collectivism is an accepted political philosophy and the Welfare State is its spiritual child. Does it provide the answer to an unregulated individualism? Is it the true political anchorage? One does not need to accept Professor F. A. Hayek's conclusion that the Welfare State marks 'the road to Serfdom', but one must assert that all forms of society lack absolute validity; all come under judgement. In the case of the planned society the canons of criticism are three. Is it politically, economically, and spiritually able to subserve its true function of making possible the good life for all its citizens?

First of all there must be an adequate political philosophy. The root objection to individualism is that, in A. D. Lindsay's phrase, a man 'is reduced to a bundle of pleasures or desires and the State to a collection of atoms'; there is no inner principle of coherence. This however cannot be secured by changing the State into a 'great leviathan'. Then the remedy is worse than the disease. The parts must not dwarf the whole, but neither must the whole nullify the parts. If the individual is too strong there will be anarchy, if the State is too strong there will be despotism.

> *O! it is excellent*
> *To have a giant's strength, but it is tyrannous*
> *To use it like a giant.*[3]

What must be the proper relationship between the State and its subjects? The answer depends upon the true function of the State and the readiness of the individual to serve that function. Twentieth-century thinking and writing on this subject has been greatly influenced by the Oxford School of Idealists whose greatest figure, T. H.

---

[3] *Measure for Measure*, II. ii. 107.

Green, died in 1882. In his famous *Lectures on the Principles of Political Obligation*, he chose as a title for one of his lectures: 'Will, not force, is the Basis of the State.' From the seventeenth-century Puritans, as well as from Kant and Rousseau, T. H. Green and his school derived their belief in the worth and dignity of the ordinary man. The State depends for its working upon the consent of the governed. There must therefore be 'the idea of a common good which the State fulfils'. Green does not contest the fact of individual liberties, but he argues that 'liberties are of no use or have no meaning except in relation to a good for which they are used'. Any theory of the State as an organism may seem to justify State absolutism, but Green saved himself by reference to that larger moral good which State and individual must alike conserve.

In the light of this philosophy he discusses in what sense the individual has rights against the State and the State against the individual. He concludes, as a good Hegelian, that in so far as the State pursues a right moral goal, the aims of the individual and the Government ought to be identical. There is no need on the one side for the use of arbitrary force, nor on the other for the naked assertion of individual rights. This confluence of public and personal interests implies an organic conception of the State. It is not an aggregation of private persons, but neither has it the monolithic unity of a single will. It is the organized society of those who find an identity of interest in their pursuit of the common good. T. H. Green never discarded Rousseau's '*volonté générale*', but he gave it a new twist of meaning. In his discussion on *Sovereignty and the General Will*, he disallowed the presuppositions flowing from the idea of natural rights; but if he refused to acknowledge a right against Society, he welcomed the right to be treated as a member of Society. 'A right', he said, 'is a power claimed and recognized as contributing to the common good.' It was in this sense of the individual's participation in the State that he advocated the general will in the service of the common good.

If this can be taken as a working definition of political society, it follows that individuals within the State must conceive themselves as members within the body politic. Here is a flash-back to Edmund Burke's conception of the State as the 'living partnership' of the governed. There is no longer room for individualism or totalitarianism. There is only the call to exercise the rights of the private member in the interests of the whole body. This was not the first time such a clarion note had been sounded. Mazzini had protested to his Italian co-patriots: 'There are no rights but duties!' The great President

Thomas Jefferson asserted similarly that 'there are no private rights but only public duties'. Such assertion now had additional force, because they derived from a formulated philosophy of the State. After Green's early death, D. G. Ritchie, Edward Caird, Bernard Bosanquet, and William Wallace sustained his work. F. H. Bradley, who was an influential later member of the school, wrote in his *Ethical Studies* a section with the strangely significant title: 'My Station and its Duties.'

It is this balanced collectivism which must underpin the Welfare State. This is the political canon by which to judge a State's effectiveness. Not that the standard is easy in practice to apply! A nation is made up of many groups, and how is a man to regulate his loyalties between his family, his work, the community, and the nation? It was Laird in *The Idea of Value* who said that 'social enterprises need to be justified as much as individual enterprises'. In his book on F. H. Bradley, Dr W. F. Lofthouse faces this difficulty. He argues that love to a husband must take a different course from love to a business rival, an enemy of the State, or a habitual criminal, and 'the practical difficulty of realizing oneself in a society of opposing elements may shake the foundations of the noblest theory'. T. H. Green himself was aware that his organic theory of the State did not mean the citizen could expect detailed guidance in his conduct. The citizen, he argued, had no rule of right (in the strict sense of the word) to guide him. What then did he have? Green answered: 'The general rule of looking to the moral good of mankind, to which a necessary means is the organization of the State.' In his *Testament of Beauty*, Robert Bridges wrote two lines which are an apt comment on such advice:

> *In that uncharted jungle a good man wil go right,*
> *while an ill disposition wil miss and go wrong.*

If the theory still seems vague in its present-day application, it is not because of muddy thinking, but because in its moral idealism it demands for its working an educated and enlightened democracy. Certain assumptions it takes for granted. There must be the fullest use of local and national privileges in the exercise of one's citizenship. It was the Irishman, John Philpot Curran, who declared that 'the condition upon which God hath given liberty to man is eternal vigilance'. Citizenship means infinitely more than the casting of a vote. It involves conscious participation in the affairs of the State. It will mean statutory service for some, voluntary service for many, but active interest on the part of all. A Welfare State becomes a bureau-

E

cracy if its affairs are in the hands of its civil servants and public officials. What could be worse ultimately than an active band of salaried servants and the passive army of recipients?

The common jibe against the Welfare State is that it is the 'Universal Provider'. To vary the metaphor, it holds a gigantic umbrella protecting all its little ones from the rain. The only preservative against such a peril is the active enforcement of the general will, the co-operation of all citizens in the far ends of a moral good which the State exists to conserve.

This involves the readiness to pay one's taxes cheerfully, recognizing that they are not a burden to be borne grudgingly, but a responsibility of citizenship to be accepted willingly. They are then understood as a fiscal application of 'bearing one another's burdens'. It also means that there can be no assertion of one's own rights against the State. If my own political party is not in power, I have the duty of supporting the opposition and of making my own view-point clear in the circles where I have influence; I have no right to discredit without due reason those who are in power and to withhold my full support from State policies until my own party is again in authority. In a word, the lesser political loyalty must be contained within the greater. A similar principle applies to economic groupings. It is entirely right for the worker to be a member of his appropriate Trade Union; he has, in many instances, attained his present standards of labour because of the struggle of Trade Unionism in the past, and there may be present advantages to be attained through the solidarity of members within the same Trade Union. What cannot be justified is the strike initiated by Communist influence and having the purely negative end of dislocating the smooth working of a nation's industrial life. Nor can a strike be tolerated which is due to a sudden upsurge of private interests damaging to the public interests, or which is embarked on without any proper recourse to the full machinery of negotiation and arbitration. In more countries than one, a strike has often the appearance of a 'try-out'. Because the nation is exposed to serious inconvenience and possible hardship, the strikers hope that their claim will be conceded, careless of whether it is justified or not! This is economic blackmail, and it rests on the harmful theory that private interests can be pressed ruthlessly even when they conflict with the general good. Finally a strike is to be condemned when it is an industrial civil war between Unions in which the public at large are the innocent sufferers. It may be argued that one cannot generalize on particular cases, and that by bringing grievances into the open they can be better remedied. But the fight between a smaller and a larger Union, or two fairly equal Unions, whose interests overlap is of such vital and painful interest to the community that a better procedure than public war to the death must be found.

The argument might seem to imply that all strikes ought to be considered illegal. On the contrary, except in totalitarian countries the right to strike in the last resort has been conceded. But as in any private or group opposition to the public interests, the strikers must show that it is not the selfish unjustified action of a certain industrial section, but a grave unavoidable step, satisfying the ends of justice and therefore justifiable in a State which professes to seek the common good of its members.

We have been mainly considering working-class interests which may conflict with national policy. The argument holds equally for other social classes within the community. The rich are often the powerful, and by monopolistic and restrictive practices they can hold a community to ransom; the many are sacrificed that the few may be richer still. There can also be the wrongful evasion of taxation or the clever manipulation of market fluctuations to bring off a private gamble at a public cost. Any such assertion of private or class interests against the common good is as blameworthy on the part of the management as on that of the worker side of industry.

Whether one is thinking in political, economic, or social terms, the same principle must be applied. Rights must be conceived as duties. A man or a class within a nation can never stand outside that community to which they owe, in a material sense, their very existence. They have a right to pursue their rights, but only as they are able to show that in a real sense their protest is ultimately for the common good. The Welfare State demands the active co-operation of its members. There is a public interest which transcends all private interests, and there must be a general will, in the idealistic sense of the term, which actively seeks the good of the State, a good which benefits both the State and its members.

There is a second canon of judgement which turns the searchlight upon the economic theory and practice of a nation. Capitalism is a word with emotional overtones. By association of ideas it recalls for many people the most degrading features of nineteenth-century industrialism, when conditions of labour were intolerably severe, and women and children suffered most of all. They dismiss it as a vile system in which capital is concentrated in private hands for the pursuit of private interests and the many are thereby sacrificed for the few. The phrase 'dark satanic mills' wholly conforms to their mental picture. The most highly industrialized nation of the nineteenth century was Great Britain, and in its worst period there were the boy chimney-sweeps, the half-naked women chained to their coal-trucks, and the long toilsome hours that children worked in factories under harsh supervision. Towns sprang up without intelligent planning, the maximum number of houses was built in the space available. Back-to-back houses were a common feature of the builders' misguided ingenuity, and in these wretched slums workers found that 'two ha'p'orth of gin' was the quickest way out of the depressing tedium of their existence.

Even in Great Britain, however, this was the situation in its most sombre colours, and in other countries capitalism was never so grim and forbidding. The black-and-white contrasts were rather to be found in non-industrial countries like Egypt and Iran, where a few land-owners had great wealth and many of the population were steeped in age-long poverty, ignorance, and despair.

Throughout the last century capitalism was passing through many phases, so that today there is no modern State in which capitalism in its pure dictionary-meaning exists. Where can one find a great nation in which capital is wholly gathered in private hands? In 'capitalist' countries there can be every graduation from the private tradesman, and the one-owner undertaking, to the company of limited liability, the combine, and various forms of State management, control, or ownership. To condemn capitalism as an economic theory may be a nice academic exercise, but to condemn it in practice is to use the word without strict significance. Edmund Burke said, 'I do not know a method of drawing up an indictment against a whole people', and 'capitalism' is now one of those words which cover so much ground that they forbid generalizations. It is not possible to frame a coherent charge against a whole system, a system that contains within itself every stage between private and State control.

Nevertheless many are incapable of judging capitalism in this dispassionate way. The connotation of the word for them will always be a system of free and private enterprise. Because their reaction is primarily emotional, they treat the word in this doctrinaire fashion, and fire their bullets at a phantom. The greater their dislike of 'capitalism' the more inclined they are to advocate 'socialism', which in their uncomplicated thinking seems to stand in contrast to the dark foe as a veritable angel of light. Despite their seeming progressiveness they live in a medieval atmosphere of knight errantry. They may

or may not be interested in good and evil in a moral sense, but
they are profoundly convinced of it in the world of economics. The
more they are convinced of the total depravity of the 'capitalist'
and his system, the more fervent is their advocacy of its complete
opposite.

That is why Marx, Lenin, and Stalin denounced capitalism as the
old-time preacher denounced the devil, and proceeded logically to
suppose that total deliverance would only come from whole-hogged
State ownership. Take capital out of private into public hands, and
darkness turns to light. The excesses of Communism are so patent
that even fellow-travellers can have their mental reservations. Nevertheless many ardent reformers, whose love of the brethren is shown by
hatred of their masters, still believe in that classic Socialist aim of the
State—control of the means of production, distribution, and exchange.
This, of course, is to forfeit the lessons of economic history for a
formula. If capitalism in its earliest form of total private enterprise is
one extreme, then socialism in this definition is the other extreme and
equally to be condemned. It is a severe emotional reaction from
manifest injustice and greed; but it is quite unreal.

Nationalization as a creed suffers from a naïve belief in the virtue of
the State as distinguished from the vice of private citizens, as though
the defects of the individual were miraculously transmitted into the
orderly capacity of the organized whole. Life is not so tidy. There is
no superhuman entity called a State possessing a perfected mental
instrument and able therefore to take over blundering private enterprises and make them marvellously efficient.

It was that ardent British Socialist, Sir Stafford Cripps, who said,
'There must be no control for control's sake', 'no planning for the
sake of planning'. In that same vein of argument there must not be
wholesale nationalization for the sake of nationalization. In this age of
collectivism it is not socialism which is to be feared, but that Utopian
adherence to an idea which elevates a theory into a moral crusade.

There are three general tests to be applied before any enterprise is
taken out of private into public hands. The first test is one of historical inevitability. In the march of events a certain combination of circumstances clearly indicates that one course of action is to be preferred. So in Great Britain as elsewhere a time came when public
utilities such as gas, water, electricity, were taken over by the State.
This 'gas and water socialism' would not now offend the most con-
servatively minded. Later in Great Britain railways and coal-mines
came in the same way under public ownership. In some other

countries there is a parallel movement through subsidy and control to nationalization.

Secondly there is the test of economic expediency. There is no case for taking over an enterprise which is highly profitable and serves well both the interests of its employers and the country as a whole. It is asking little to demand that no enterprise be nationalized unless there is excellent reason to suppose that economically it will be more profitable under State management than in private hands. There is no virtue in maintaining an economic doctrinaire purity even though State ownership spells loss. This can only be justfied on moral grounds.

So finally there is the test of moral justification. If a monopoly becomes so gigantic in its operation and so self-regarding in its profit-making that the public interest is imperilled, there is a clear case first for public control and later, if necessary, for public ownership. Under this moral test must also be considered the vested interests in harmful commodities. There are certain undertakings such as the trade in gambling or in alcoholic liquor which are so anti-social in their cumulative effects that they call for the strictest fiscal, judicial, and administrative control. Here the demand is not that they should be taken over by the State, but limited in their capacity to do public hurt.

Where these tests are applied satisfactorily, then not for the sake of nationalization, but for the country's good, let an undertaking come into public hands. The health of a country demands that there shall be both public and private enterprise. There is a place for the tradesman, the shopkeeper, the private employer, the limited company, the State undertaking. If there is to be a correlation of the parts and the whole in the service of the common good, there must be worthy scope for individual and group initiative. There is also a proper place for governmental control and ownership. The relative parts one assigns to State or individual will depend upon one's political alignments. The all-important conclusion is that neither individualism nor collectivism is good enough. In a dynamic conception of the State, private interests will not be allowed to prejudice the common good, nor will the State dwarf individual aspiration; there will be, through public and private action, an economic identity of interest which will be in the nation's highest good.

The last of the great canons of judgement is religious in character: the Welfare State must never be regarded as the god out of the machine. Reformers have toiled for a planned society, and spoken of it so eloquently that many have supposed that with its advent the earthly

Utopia would arrive. The supposition is that once people are freed from want, insecurity, and ignorance, and are allowed to enjoy a good standard of living, they will ask no more. To argue in these terms, however, is to suppose that man can be perfectly satisfied in a spacee time order. It is simply not true. Here is a pet poodle in a woman's arms. No special gift is necessary to reconstruct that doggie's life. It will sleep in a comfortable chair; it will feed on the choicest morsels; it will be combed and brushed and shampooed and endlessly petted. It will know a doggie's paradise. And if we are the pet poodles of creation, then feed us, clothe us, pet us, keep us free from draughts, and nothing else will we require. But if 'we look before and after' and 'pine for what is not', we cannot be wholly satisfied with the things that are. A healthy mind in a healthy body was a Roman ideal that needs considerable expansion of meaning to meet the complex needs of man.

The proof of that lies in the spiritual condition of modern society. There are common phrases such as 'I haven't a clue' or 'I couldn't care less' which must have their parallel in other languages. Ivor Brown has complained that 'frustration' is a much over-used word. But the word is used so much because people feel frustrated. Despite the endless gadgets tossed on to their laps, they are bored and restless and unsatisfied. Indeed the matter goes farther than that. Mental Hospitals are overcrowded, the clinics of the psychiatrists are filled with anxious seekers for mental health. The characteristic illness of the age is 'nerves', and the sign and symbol of the modern era is the aspirin tablet. Amongst the best sellers of the day are books which give clues to 'positive living' and show how to attain 'peace of mind'. Part of the romantic interest in interstellar space and adventures with peoples from other worlds is the desire to escape the tensions of this particular planet.

Another symptom of this inner dissatisfaction is the success of the great mass-evangelists. Let the utmost credit be given to the personality and message of the people concerned and to the excellence of their organization. The vast number of hearers, and the size of the response, still betoken a great hunger of spirit. For a variety of reasons people at large are not willing to find spiritual satisfaction in the worship and sacraments of the historic Churches. The need however still remains, and so mass evangelism has taken a new and ever more vigorous lease of life. The basic formula of the evangelist is very simple. You are a divided creature and nothing that the world can give will meet your real needs. In your sin you need a Saviour. God is willing to forgive you and to keep you day by day. Are you willing to let Him? The success of the message lies in the fact that it speaks to the true condition of men. At its best, a Government can remove abuses and supply the right conditions for the good life; it cannot supply the good life itself. It has no power to forgive sins, to deliver men from the thraldom of evil habits, to sustain them on their pilgrimage. It can offer no answers to the most pressing questions of all; it cannot tell a man who he is, what he has to do, where he must go, and what awaits him at the end of his journey.

The State that tries to impose itself on the individual as the 'be-all and end-all of life' is 'the abomination of desolation'. In its assumptions it does violence to the spirit of man. On the other hand, an individual who seeks to find his full life within the State is subject to perpetual frustration. Unless he recognizes the limits of a State, what it can do and what lies for ever beyond its capacity, he is doomed to despair. There is a need of men which can be met by God alone. This is the temporal justification for the place of the Church within the State. Deny that place, hinder the Church's working, restrict its freedom of movement and propaganda, and the State itself is weakened. In the play *Glorious Morning* the mode of greeting was to say: 'The State is all.' The girl who died because she refused to deny allegiance to One greater than the State may stand as a symbol for those who recognize that the true life of man is lived at once within the State and above it. He is a citizen of two countries and must needs acknowledge his debt to both.

In this last canon, as in the other two, the judgement is made that the right to worship should be conceived as a duty. Further, the demand is made that the ends of the State and of the individual within it should coincide. It is in the truest welfare of State and citizen alike that God's name shall be hallowed, His Kingdom be sought, and His will be done on earth as it is in heaven.

CHAPTER VI

ANTIDOTE TO TYRANNY

COLLECTIVISM is a word which in one particular resembles a bulldog's face: it is ugly but expressive. It draws immediate attention to the whole rather than the part, to the State rather than the individual. For a hundred years this has been the main emphasis in political thinking. If the unprivileged, the workers, the sick, and the aged, are to be helped, it can be only through the steady expansion of the State's authority. Individuals contribute through various forms of insurance, but the control of the money and its dispensation belongs to the State. The growth of the Welfare State has therefore in another aspect been the growth in power of the State.

This tendency has been strengthened by three other factors. Firstly, the rapid expansion of trade, the scramble for world markets, and the need for capital in large overseas investment, has introduced the State as a gigantic figure in the world of buying and selling. This authority has sometimes been exercised through a control of the volume of imports and exports. It may in times of emergency amount to specific directions regarding what is sold abroad and what is allowed for the home market. Always, by its system of tariffs and other forms of taxation, a nation can determine the flow and nature of imports. In recent years there has also been the emergence of the State as a buyer and a seller in bulk. In times of war this control of trade has been almost complete, and once a nation has thus known absolute powers of economic determination, its hold over the nation's economy only slowly and reluctantly relaxes.

Side by side with this increasing power over its country's overseas trade, the modern State has vastly strengthened its hold over internal economy. In many countries, through appropriate Governmental ministries, through the instrument of taxation, and through various forms of State control and ownership, there has been a tight hold over commerce and industry. Economically, therefore, the modern State has swollen to the size of Hobbes's *Leviathan*.

Even more remarkable has been the second factor in the State's increase of power—namely, science. When a revolt is successful it is called a revolution; when it is unsuccessful it is called a conspiracy. Modern revolts have almost always been conspiracies. There are two great modern exceptions. The cries of 'Liberty, Equality, and Fraternity' were sufficient to bring down the walls of the French

Jericho. But this only occurred because the State had lost its executive authority, and could no longer command the allegiance of its armies. When in its weakness the Government allowed the insurgent middle classes to arrogate power to themselves, the end was certain. In the same way, the Czarist régime collapsed in Russia because its armies had been decisively defeated. There was left no strong centralized authority. Instead, the country drifted helplessly like a ship without a rudder. In March 1917 local strikes and mass demonstrations of hunger-maddened people merged into a general strike and enormous political rallies. Soldiers crossed over to the side of the very workers they were sent to intimidate. A council of workers and soldiers was formed in Petrograd and then came the mutiny of the Black Sea and Baltic fleets. The revolt had become a revolution. This was not due primarily to the fact that Lenin was smuggled into Russia and at once took the initiative. Of himself he was powerless, but in a situation where the State had lost its authority and could not even control its own forces, he was able to seize the tiller and direct the ship of State.

It has therefore always been important for the State to gather military force into its own hands. Circumstances have driven home the truth that such control is vital to its very existence. But the modern developments in high-explosive bombs, poison-gases, military aircraft, and nuclear fission, have given sharp and added significance to the fact that no scientific discoveries of the slightest military importance can ever be left to individuals and groups; they must immediately come under State control. This means that both military forces and the armaments they use are directly under the direction of the Government concerned. Scientists may have private lives, but they have a public allegiance and responsibility. Both the military and peaceful uses of atomic energy are entirely controlled by the State. In any emergency, martial law secures its complete hold over public life. How remote therefore is the chance of a successful revolt, unless by external circumstances a country's executive authority has been dangerously weakened. Modern scientific progress has made the State into a Colossus.

The third factor is less tangible. Its roots are in psychology, but its consequences are in politics. The twentieth century has been the century of wars, but of wars with a difference. In former times the serving men belonged to a professional class, and unless the country was actually invaded the civilian population only saw the war at one remove. Even the numbers engaged were relatively small and their capacity for mutual destruction was relatively limited. Significantly, the two wars of this century have been called World Wars I and II. This has underlined the global nature of modern warfare. Once a war breaks out between great Powers, the consequences involve all mankind. Another distinctive feature of twentieth-century war is that weapons of mass destruction have been employed with ever greater effectiveness. At this present moment we stand irresolutely on the edge of a precipice, because the Hydrogen Bomb and its further progeny imperil the whole future of man.

One of the slogans in World War I calculated to move the heart of the allied combatants declared: 'We must make the world safe for democracy.' Tyranny was to be overthrown that men might be free. In the event, the precise opposite happened. Germany was indeed defeated, but both sides were so exhausted spiritually as well as materially that the prevailing mood was of apathy and not of eager confident idealism.

When men have received a great shock, and are frightened and insecure, they are more ready than ever to fly to the all-enclosing embrace of the State. They are willing to surrender their own power if the State may thereby become all-powerful. The individual decreases that the State may increase. The underlying assumption is that only the strong man strongly armed can keep his goods in peace. The State becomes *'ein' feste Burg'* and offers its strength as a protection to those who have surrendered their liberties. Even in the victor States this seemed a fair bargain. None of the Democracies was so 'democratic' in the technical sense once the war was over. They had acquired powers which they only reluctantly and partly surrendered. Indeed one reason why the League of Nations ultimately foundered is that States refused to surrender any part of their national sovereignty in the cause of a world society.

In the defeated, this same process of reasoning was more evident and more extreme. Russians, in their sense of weakness and insecurity, accepted the strong rule of the Bolsheviks. The 'little father', Czar Nicholas, had been unable to save them; many had been exposed to the wintry blasts of war, poverty, hunger, disillusionment, and defeat. Now perhaps comrade Lenin had the answer. Communism had begun to make history.

In like manner the Germans at the close of the war were in a trauma. From an arrogance begotten by a sense of superiority they had fallen abruptly into depths of shame, confusion, and despair. If the convalescence was to lead to recovery of mental health they needed sympathetic and understanding treatment from victor nations. They needed help supremely in their experiment in democracy during the days of the Weimar republic. These conditions were not fulfilled and Germany was ripe psychologically for the arrival of a Hitler. In the strong State, he promised the sure refuge his people needed; in his treatment of the Jews, a scapegoat was provided for the people's sins; in the fresh assertion of national power, the feeling of inferiority could again give place to a recovered self-respect.

Italy, technically, was on the winning side, but her wounds had been so grievous and her internal condition so chaotic that Italians also were ready to welcome any leader who would restore authority and order. They did not find it difficult to subordinate their individual selves if they thought Fascism could bring security, dignity, and a new national greatness. Any survey of post-war Europe shows that the world had become dangerously unsafe for democracy. Out of the shocks of war, insecure and fear-ridden people have allowed the State to grow in political power. Already the operation of economic, scientific, and political factors has resulted in the strong nation. An urgent question arises: Can the process be stopped? Can there still be a working combination of individual freedom and initiative with an efficient centralized authority? Is order consistent with liberty? Can the State be powerful and its citizens not suffer? All these questions are but variants of the one question. Is totalitarianism in some form inevitable?

The answer depends upon whether the Christian valuation of the State is accepted or rejected. In his book *The Public Philosophy*, Walter Lippmann has made a strong plea for a restatement of the concept of natural law which can form the basis of a public philosophy. He argues that only in a reference both to general principles and particular circumstances can liberal democracy and tolerance exist. He wants a new sense of urgency and responsibility in political actions. Almost, he would desire the religious sense of awe as men approach their political tasks. But that cannot be secured on his own premises. Even men's belief that they are upholders of natural law will not produce the same holy dread that comes on those who know the truth behind the dominical saying: 'He that falleth on this stone shall be broken to pieces: but on whomsoever it shall fall, it will scatter him as dust.' As Mr T. E. Utley, writing in the *Spectator* (10th June 1955), acutely observed: 'What liberal democratic theory needs to supplement it is a sense of the day of judgement.' The first and the last State reference must therefore be to God.

Francis Bacon declared that the four pillars of government were religion, justice, counsel, and treasure. Religion, although it comes first on his list, does not mean that citizens must be religious. This is a 'consummation devoutly to be wished', but the art of government does not wait for it. It does however necessitate the acceptance of Christian social principles. There is no systematic teaching in the New Testament on the State, but there are the data for a Christian philosophy. The *locus classicus* is in Paul's letter to the Romans (Chapter 13). The State is the servant of God. No Jew willingly surrendered the idea of the true nation as a theocracy. Even though earthly rulers were permitted, they were answerable to God. Divine permission depended on their sense of commission. In the wisdom of Solomon rang the cry: 'Give ear ye that rule the people and glory in the multitude of nations. For power is given you of the Lord, and sovereignty from the Highest, who shall try your works and search out your counsels.'

The State is answerable to God in three main functions: it must preserve peace and order, it must remove the hindrances to social well-being, and it must create the right conditions for the good life. From the account of the Temptation in the Wilderness, it would seem that Jesus recognized that the downward drag in human nature was reflected in social institutions. Nevertheless He ordered tribute money to be paid to the civil authorities and He declared that to Caesar must be rendered his proper dues. There is an echo of this dominical saying in Paul's injunction to 'Render to all their dues: tribute to whom tribute is due; custom to whom custom; fear to whom fear; honour to whom honour'. Paul enjoined loyal submission to the State because it did preserve peace and order. The *pax Romana* not only kept the barbarian outside the frontier defences, but it suppressed lawlessness and brigandage within the Empire. Time and again Paul owed his life to the timely intervention of Roman officials and soldiers. Further, Roman rule guaranteed justice to its citizens. It was, in his own words, a 'terror' only to the evil doer. The law-abiding citizen had nothing to fear: 'Do that which is good and thou shalt have praise of the same.'

If the ruler is above the law, or in legal terms, if the executive raises itself above the legislature, then the State becomes a tyranny dispensing justice according to the notions of the rulers and their puppets. There must be a system of law binding upon all. Only so can justice be done and order be preserved. For the maintenance of order does not depend only upon the executive's adequate authority, but upon its willingness to abide by a recognized and accepted body of law.

In so far as the State is 'an avenger for wrath', it is ready to deal appropriately with private and social evils. The definition of evil is not, however, to be left to the State, or once again despotism will rear an ugly head. It would justify the most arbitrary self-interested actions on the part of the Government. Evil is that which is condemned by natural law. This wider working of God in His universe is lit up and interpreted in the Christian revelation. The State is no guardian of a man's conscience. It will not proceed against him for deceitfulness, lying, covetousness, or any other private failing. When, however, his wrong-doing is hurtful to society, then in the interests of society the State will take action.

The punishment inflicted in the name of the State will not be a deterrent only; it will also be remedial and reformative. The aim will be not only the protection of society but the reclamation of the wrong-doer himself.

This negative aspect of the State's function covers also the removal of hindrances to the good life. In the early-nineteenth century this was construed in England as meaning that the State must keep its hands off the individual. The underlying assumption was that a man is the best judge of his own welfare. The less the State interferes, therefore, the more the common good is secured. The only justifiable interference was the removal of the restrictions on individual freedom. In this way the small property-holders, and finally, the ordinary citizen, received a vote; workmen secured the right to combine in Unions, and Dissenters were freed from their disabilities. No State properly functions unless the elementary rights of the individual as a responsible being are secured. He must have freedom of speech, worship, and association; he must have freedom from unlawful arrest and imprisonment, and the right of defence when charged. Only when he is free can he be accountable for his actions and therefore responsible to his fellows. If he is handicapped by sickness, old age, disablement, or unemployment, the State must interfere on his behalf so that he is not unduly handicapped in that race of life which all perforce must run.

The removal of hindrances, however, is more than the removal of restrictions on freedom. Shaftesbury's labours to secure the Ten Hours Act for industrial workers is an illustration of the way in which the State can remedy intolerable grievances. In a like manner, a long series of Acts improved the lot of woman and child, the factory-hand, the shop-assistant, and the agricultural labourer. Whenever people suffer because of the conditions of their employment, the State has a right and duty to intervene. The better treatment accorded to the insane, the prisoner, and the dumb animal is a welcome sign that the State growingly recognizes its right to protect even those who cannot speak for themselves.

These are illustrations of the prophet's word that in the desert there should be prepared a highway for our God. To do that, it is necessary first that the tangled undergrowth be removed so that a road may be built. Any valid interpretation of Christian social principles asserts that the State, as God's minister, must perform what might appear to be negative tasks in the light of a positive ideal. Weeds must not be allowed to grow in the same garden as flowers.

Yet even as hindrances are swept away, the right conditions for living the good life must be well established. Welfare legislation which benefits family life, which secures the best conditions for industry, which provides fullest educational opportunities, which preserves the rights of minorities in community life, which recognizes no social religious or colour bar in its provision of equal opportunities for all its citizens, and which respects the convictions of the individual conscience—accords with the State's positive function as the servant of God. It cannot confer the good life, but it can by its legislation fulfil the end of the State as expressed by William Temple: 'The State exists for the citizen, not the citizen for the State. The first aim of social progress must be to give the fullest possible scope for the exercise of all powers and qualities which are distinctly personal.'

What, in sum, does this Christian valuation of the State signify? It determines its status, its functions, and its objective. It declares the accountability of rulers to God, and therefore their responsibility to their people. No State exists in its own right, upheld by its own power, and answerable to itself alone. Absolute power belongs to God alone; all else is derivative and must be used in trust. The State therefore may ask for obedience, but not worship. It is not God, but a servant of God, and can only demand allegiance when it is faithful to its trust. The writer of the Revelation of St John did not hesitate, during a time of persecution and terror, to speak of the Roman Empire as the 'Beast'. The Christian religion in its thought and practice has consistently maintained the individual right to oppose the State if it acts contrary to God's intention. The status of earthly rulers is subordinate to the heavenly Ruler; He is the King of kings and the Lord of lords.

From this conception of status follows the nature of the State's function. It must 'hinder the hindrances' to public well-being, even as it makes it more easy for the good life to be lived. In the exercise of these functions it has the enrichment of individual life as its constant objective. In this respect John Stuart Mill's essay on liberty is not outdated. His argument ran to the conclusion that 'the worth of a State is the worth of the individuals who compose it'. In memorable words he declared that 'a State which dwarfs its men in order that they may be more docile instruments in its hands, even for beneficial purposes, will find that with small men no great thing can be accomplished.' The end of the State, therefore, is the encouragement of men to be great and not small, to be free and not slaves. It intends men actively to enjoy the good life and not passively to receive a substitute.

In order that the individual may be served by the State and society treated as a community of responsible people, free institutions must be preserved and respected. In Government there must be the right of unfettered opposition, even to the degree of paying a salary to the leader of Her Majesty's Opposition—as in the British Parliament. There must be the healthy criticism made possible by a free Press. It was Junius who declared in his *Letters* that 'the liberty of the Press is "the Palladium of all the civil, political, and religious rights of an Englishman" '. The assertion applies with equal force in any country. Muzzle the Press and you gag the citizen. Men must be free to write, to propagate their views, to own private property, and to associate together in industry and society. Since the modern State is essentially bureaucratic, its health depends not only on the efficiency of statutory bodies, but on the quality and variety of its voluntary bodies. These are recognized conditions for the flowering of individuals into persons, living together as members of the same organized society.

Most important of all is the right to worship and to witness. 'We are ready', said Cavour in 1861, 'to proclaim throughout Italy the great principle of a free Church in a free State.' That principle is still essential to a State which would serve the ends of all its members.

The individual must respect the authority of the State and yet safeguard his own proper place in the life of society. Even more, the Church must be a continual check upon the State, working out in public life and thought the implications of a teaching which is at once a preservative against absolutism and a vindication of the importance of the common man. It cannot be too strongly insisted that, even though the State discharges its functions as the servant of God, and though it maintains the right equilibrium between State and citizen it still cannot confer the good life.

If we insist on the justice the State must dispense, the functions it must exercise, and the objective it must keep in view, we must equally insist upon the things it cannot do. Eternal life is the gift of God. Forgiveness, deliverance, renewal are not within the resources of any State. No State can make possible a peace passing understanding, a power that can remove mountains. It is a popular modern heresy that when we get what science and politics seek to give we shall have attained the land of heart's desire, and body, mind, and spirit will be equally satisfied. The reasoning is almost as naïve as the Marxist dream of the classless society. It seems to be assumed that when we have come into our modern Utopia, we shall have left behind lust, cruelty, selfishness, and driving ambition. Jesus spoke of tares and wheat growing together, but optimists can predict a field of golden grain. It is an altogether superficial estimate of human nature.

Ideally the Church in its corporate life stands above the strife of party politics, but it remains the conscience of the community, approving the good and denouncing the evil in public life. As salt, it is a pungent preservative against corruption. As light, it gives both guidance and direction in the ordering of the common life. As leaven, it quickens the whole with its own spiritual vitality.

The Church recognizes that the Kingdom of God is not eating and drinking or any other material comforts. It is beyond the reach of the technical resources of man. It is righteousness and peace and joy in the Holy Ghost. These are gifts to be received and not rewards to be earned. They come from God alone. When the State has done all, the good life itself can only be enjoyed as a gift. It is given to those who ask. To the Church has been given the proclamation of this Gospel. The story of Abraham is a continual reminder that those best build an earthly city who seek a city which hath foundations, whose builder and maker is God.

F

CHAPTER VII

THE COMMUNIST CHALLENGE

THE assumption that a due balance must be maintained between order and freedom, and that this can best be secured in a social democracy, is hotly denied by multitudes. Since Communists persist in using the word democracy for themselves, it is necessary to distinguish between individualistic democracy in which the main emphasis is still on personal freedom and the minimum of State influence, social democracy in which is sought the proper balance between State and individual action, and State democracy in which the stress is wholly on the State and its untrammelled right to interfere. During this century we have already witnessed the rise and fall of two totalitarian systems. One was based on race and the other on class, but both were in fact personal dictatorships and were doomed to disintegrate with the fall of their leaders.

Communism is altogether different, because it depends not on any single man, but on a closely articulated programme for living. Others therefore can dip their torches into the flame on Russian altars and carry the fire to the Balkans, to China, to South Eastern Asia, and in time (Russian Communists believe), to the remaining countries of the world. It is indeed the great missionary creed of the twentieth century. It is a mere academic exercise to point out the economic fallacies of Marxism. It has been done most ably and convincingly by many, and yet Communism marches on. Riddle with bullets the Marxian theory of labour as the source of value, labour-time as the measurement value, and Capitalism as the exploitation of surplus value, and behold, the citadel of Communism is still not taken.

It is possible to come to grips with Communism only when one acknowledges it is not just an economic theory or a social philosophy, but a faith devoutly held. It is, of course, sheer nonsense to describe it as a Christian heresy. A system that has no place for God, let alone the revelation of Himself in Jesus Christ, is not a deviation from Christianity; it is a totally different and alternative interpretation of life. It is true that some woolly-thinking, if enthusiastic, Christian social reformers have been so enthralled by their view of certain aspects of Communist economics and social practice that they have looked on it as a 'realized brotherhood'. Some have even believed, despite all the evidence, that Christianity and Communism were compatible, and that a man could profess both faiths at the same time. To such lengths can credulity go. The one tincture of common sense in this position is the recognition that Communism is a faith. It is a faith because it offers the believer a Cause, greater than himself, for which he must live and if necessary die. It offers him a way to tread and a goal to beckon him on his pilgrimage. He is given the inestimable satisfaction of knowing that 'history is on his side', and that in the consummation of history, when the classless society emerges, his faith will be triumphantly vindicated.

To understand the main elements in this creed it is necessary to know the main sources of inspiration in the thought of Karl Marx. He had three teachers, who between them supplied a set of ideas which were fused and integrated in his own thinking.

First of all he was profoundly indebted to Ludwig Feuerbach, a minor German philosopher with a major influence. In the first half of the nineteenth century in Germany, he was the most forthright and uncompromising atheist. This did not mean that he was also a complete materialist. In his *Commentary on Communism*, Edward Rogers has shown that he was a 'doughty opponent of crude materialism'.[1] Nevertheless he had no place at all for the idea of God. In his *Religion* he declared that 'Gods are men's wishes in corporeal form'. God is a projection of man's shadow, a monstrous Brockenspiel. This means that man has only himself and his natural world to deal with. *Homo homini Deus*. No supernatural chatter is necessary. Man is what he eats! When Engels wrote his book on Feuerbach, he declared that whilst Marx fully accepted Feuerbach's main contention, he wanted to bring his abstract Man into a real Man fulfilling his true historical rôle. This was a faithful transcription of Karl Marx's own words that Feuerbach 'never arrives at active man, really existing, but always stops short at an abstract idea'. Nevertheless Feuerbach did offer a bread-and-butter philosophy of life. His conception of un-fathered man had one concrete detail. His man had a very large stomach. Once that is granted then certain practical questions arise with which Feuerbach, the philosopher, never chose to deal. A stomach must be filled. Therefore comes the struggle with other men for food. At once, therefore, the airy world of abstract thinking is left for the solid world of economics and history. Man needs food and material security. He must fight for it. What form does this struggle take?

At this point Marx turned to Hegel, his greatest teacher and the outstanding German philosopher after Immanuel Kant. Hegel, who

[1] Page 80.

died in 1831, and thus chronologically preceded Feuerbach, put man within a historical framework. He believed that history was a unity and therefore had a meaning. All is comprehended within the Absolute who is the groundwork of all existence. Temporal processes mark the unfolding of the Absolute idea. Every thought suggests, and in action produces, its opposite. There are the contrasts of heat and cold, light and darkness, inward and outward, individual and social, freedom and absolutism, yes and no. Thesis produces antithesis, and out of that conflict of ideas a new synthesis is evolved. This 'dialectic' of thought is for Hegel the developing manifestation of the Absolute. The nation State was for him the political embodiment of this process, but the ambiguity in his thought about the end of the process made it possible for Kaiser William II and Hitler to claim his teaching as the vindication of their rule.

Marx was only concerned to borrow from him the instrument of 'dialectic', and to transfer it from the realm of philosophic idealism to that of economic determination. In every age there is the struggle between man and man for the satisfaction of material wants. There are four great stages discernible in this record of domination and unwilling subjection. In this final Capitalist epoch, the *bourgeoisie* has power and the proletariat has only 'the freedom to be exploited'. Now as ever, the dialectic of history means that economic power begets rebellion and a new synthesis will emerge. What form will it take?

At this point Karl Marx quite arbitrarily decided that stage four was the final stage and that at its close would come the great *dénouement*. Instead of the development of a new complex of economic forces, there would be a violent close to dialectic history and the classless society would emerge. For such a catastrophic climax to an age-long process Karl Marx was indebted to his third great teacher, the Bible.

It is true that his father, for social reasons, had forsaken his Jewish faith for a conventional Protestantism, but the conversion was superficial. It certainly did not impress his son. By far the greater influence upon him was his Jewish ancestry and the legacy of Hebrew scriptures. This was an essential part of his mental inheritance and gave him his idea of Apocalyptic. History was not endlessly to follow an evolutionary process. Suddenly there would be climax and catastrophe. In the Old Testament and Apocrypha there was a plain statement that the age-long conflict between good and evil would be resolved dramatically by God. There would be Armageddon, but since the armies of Light were involved, the issue would not be in doubt. After the conflict would come the Millennium, and in that golden age the righteous would find reward for all their suffering. Marx took over this apparatus of ideas, making the necessary adjustments to fit his own theories. The original conception of the fight between good and evil became the struggle between *bourgeoisie* and proletariat, between the haves and have-nots. Even this distinction must not be pressed; for Marx, the fight was still essentially between good and evil. Moral values were mere abstractions until reduced to economic terms. There they had reality and significance. The Capitalist was the big bad wolf and the proletarian was the injured lamb.

Karl Marx yielded nothing to the apocalyptists in his view that the struggle would mean violence, blood, desolation, and fury. The hearts of men would fail them at the things coming to pass on the earth. The faithful, meaning always the workers, would suffer most grievously. The battle would be hardly won. Both sides would come to near exhaustion. But, with a fine disregard of logic, Marx asserted dogmatically the triumph of the workers. The expropriators would be expropriated and the reign of the saints would begin. So naïve and trusting an assumption Marx unconsciously derived from the Old Testament and Apocrypha. There, however, as in the New Testament, the victory was logically assured because it was in the line of God's purpose, and God, by very definition, can never be defeated. Marx had no such assurance; but lacking such a resting-place, he still used the language of confident faith.

In Holy Writ the Millennium is the age of blessedness unspoilt by human frailty. Here once more we have a necessary consequence of thought. If God be actively on the throne, His children need have no fear. Marx came to the same conclusion without any corresponding justification. In the classless society, forms of government would wither away. There would be no need for coercive authority. Men would not be assertive, quarrelsome, or envious, because there would not be the conditions to call such qualities forth. All would be well in that Kingdom of peace.

What solid ground had Marx for supposing that the triumph of the proletariat, however complete, would not arouse hatred and resentment in the conquered, and the dull desire for ultimate revenge, however long delayed the day of reckoning? By what authority could he postulate instead a mood of sweet reasonableness, the sloughing away of all aggressive interests, and the desire of all to live amicably as brothers?

It has been said that Marx 'invented the class war'. Most certainly his invention is a monstrous over-simplification of the reading of history. There are so many elements in history which Marx would not acknowledge. They did not fit in with his bread-and-butter theory of the struggle for life. Nevertheless, even this theory is not so perverse as its opposite. Marx could appeal to a general reading of history when he spoke of the haves and the have-nots, and the struggle for economic independence. History may be infinitely more complex and rich in its variety, but this aspect can never safely be ignored.

To speak, however, of a time when there will be no further tension and struggle is to use language that is reserved for Heaven when the spirits of just men are made perfect. Nothing is more ironic than the fact that the Marxist, who is so ruthless in his realism, uses the make-believe language of the fairy-story when he describes the idyllic conditions of the classless society. Perhaps, strictly, one ought to regard it with More's *Utopia* or Butler's *Erewhon* as an ideal community to which one may approximate but which one can never hope to realize. The Communist, however, forbids this interpretation by his insistence on a strictly literal fulfilment in history.

This is at once his strength and his weakness. It is a weakness because it does not square with human nature, and sooner or later disillusionment will come. What matters at the moment, however, is not whether it is true, but whether people believe it to be true. Men have died cheerfully for a delusion. The strength of the Marxist teaching of a classless society is that it not only vests the process of history with meaning, but actually gives history a goal. Karl Marx, thanks to his Jewish background, gave Communists not only a theory to propound, but a faith to live by. The rabble who ran through the Paris streets had never read *Le Contrat Social*, but they could repeat the slogans of Rousseau. These gave articulation to their grievances. It is not to be expected that the peasants in the Balkans or the coolies in China have read *Das Kapital*. They can, however, believe in a manifesto which says: 'Workers of the World—Unite! You have nothing to lose but your chains.' They can believe it because it closely corresponds to their condition. It is a banner waving in a battle which is their own.

Once they accept the promise Communism makes to the dispossessed, they can easily accept their struggle as part of the inevitable movement of history, and the guarantee to them and fellow-workers of a final victory. The Communist, like the Christian, has a 'sure and certain hope'; his, however, is a worldly Paradise, and it can only be achieved as the outcome of a bitter and remorseless struggle.

It is this factor which so enormously complicates the risks of war and bedevils foreign policy. In so far as Karl Marx is accepted as a prophet and his classless society as inevitable, there will be the ceaseless probing of weakness and the ruthless determination to be in the favoured position when Armageddon finally comes. In the fighting, wherever it occurs, the Communist has the assurance that he is on the winning side. He is the darling of history.

It is not therefore enough to expose the shallow, unjustified optimism about human nature. It is not enough to deny that there is a class struggle dividing humankind into two groups, and that Capitalism, involved in ever-growing contradictions, will precipitate the final conflict. It is not enough to say that in any war between Communist and non-Communist countries the issue can never be certain, but that final loss may attend us all. It is certainly not enough to dilate upon the absurdities of impossibly good people in an impossibly good society. The Communist, like the madman, follows an inner logic of his own. He is not to be frightened by our bogies. If he ever heard our analysis, which is most unlikely, he would know it was only 'lying Capitalist propaganda'.

The insistent need today is to recognize that Karl Marx gave men a faith which in essentials is easy to understand. According to his analysis man is constantly preoccupied with the struggle to live, and immemorially the weaker has been cheated and exploited by the stronger. But this will not always be so. History, by its inner processes reveals a pattern of development which favours the working man. The dialectic is moving to a climax. Then the ordinary man will enter his 'age of gold'. The Christian will want to question all these assumptions. He will object to the reducing of the rich variegated cultural pattern of history into the bare economic terms of struggle. He will ask how there can be unity and intelligibility in history without the hypotheses of God who alone can give history its unity and meaning. He will ask why Marx should assume a sudden violent end to the historical process and the triumph of the worker-saints. He will want to know why man, so divided in his nature, should after a bloody class conflict become integrated and at rest.

Such criticism is beside the point. Those who 'embrace' Communism, and the word is much better than the milder 'accept', do so in complete indifference to logic. It is for them a veritable *cri de coeur*, an irresistible appeal to a life such as they have never known, a life in which the proud are scattered and the men of low degree exalted. Whether the words of deliverance are in Russian or Chinese or an Eastern European language, the appeal is the same. There is little to lose, and so much to gain. Small wonder that Communism continues its militant march.

What ought one to do? The immediate need is not to regard the advance as a threat but a challenge. In one of his books, the late L. P. Jacks deplored the habit of calling everything a problem. Do that, he said, and you assume a wrong psychological attitude. Immediately your brows contract and you try to find the answer; don't, he argued, speak of the problems of youth or age, but of their opportunities. Regard every so-called problem as an opportunity, and what an infinitely more confident frame of mind you adopt. In this present instance one ought not to speak of the Communist problem, but of the Communist challenge, and therefore of the opportunity it presents.

This challenge is at once social, political, and religious. Communism, in whatever national dress, makes its greatest appeal to four main groups. There is the woolly-thinking idealist who longs to see the Kingdom of God established firmly in the institutions of men and who despairs of the slow-moving Churches. To him, the Communist experiment, in whatever country, is the nearest approximation to his social ideal. He believes it stands for brotherhood and does very much concretely to realize it; he is a man in a hurry, and he applauds a system of thought and action which has accomplished so much for the underdog in so short a time. Then there is the *déraciné* intellectual who applauds Communism's defiant humanism and the marked respect paid to an artist and scientist; he is impressed not so much because Communism is a democracy of the workers, but because it is an aristocracy of the *élite*. Thirdly, there is the restless discontented higher-grade worker who believes he can never gain his proper place and reward in a capitalist society, but will enter his kingdom when Communists come into power. His sentiments may be built up from bitter memories of injustice, dark prejudices inherited or begotten from early circumstances, a passionate resentment against the 'expropriators', and a present sense of failure and frustration; in a word, his may be a pathological rather than a calmly reasoned philosophy, but for that very reason it will be fiercely and tenaciously maintained. Lastly, there are the unnumbered multitudes of poorly paid workers, peasants living perpetually on the borders of starvation, and those who feel they are victimized because of their class or colour, who are potentially the good ground in which the seeds of Communism may be sown.

All these classes need to be convinced that others, apart from Communists, are interested in removing social injustice, redressing age-long grievances, and raising the general standard of living throughout the world. The social challenge is not to be accepted through fear of Communism and its onward march; nothing is done worthily which is done from a wrong motive. It is to be accepted because 'to this end' we were called. The fact of the solidarity of mankind carries with it the need of the rich to help the poor, the wise to help the ignorant, the strong to help the weak. We bear one another's burdens because we are our brothers' keepers. For our encouragement, we need to know that in the non-Communist world this lesson of living together is being slowly learnt. Out of the havoc of the war came immediate plans for wide-scale relief. At the darkest hour of the struggle, before America had entered the war, an Inter-Allied Committee on Post-War Requirements (founded September 1941) had drawn up plans for the relief and rehabilitation of the devastated areas of Europe. Later, the United States Office of foreign relief and rehabilitation operations under the control of ex-Governor Lehman worked in North Africa on the social problems arising as hostilities ended. The data and experience gained by these two bodies were invaluable when the United Nations Relief and Rehabilitation Administration (UNRRA) was established in November 1943. Forty-four Governments determined that 'immediately upon the liberation of any area by the armed forces of the United Nations or as a consequence of retreat by the enemy, the population thereof shall receive aid and relief from their sufferings, food, clothing, and shelter, aid in the prevention of pestilence, in the recovery of health of the people, and preparation and arrangements shall be made for the return of prisoners and exiles to their homes and for assistance in the resumption of urgently needed agricultural and industrial production and the restoration of essential services'.

The resolves were largely implemented in the early post-war years and the work was continued and developed by 'Marshall Aid'. This noble and imaginative plan of General Marshall, eagerly accepted by the British Foreign Secretary, Ernest Bevin, will go down in history as an altruistic act on the part of the United States, which revived the faintly beating heart of Europe and quickened her post-war recovery. It is a trite commonplace that no gratitude is to be expected in politics, and the American help given at a critical time has been dismissed by the wordly-wise as done for fear of Communist expansion. No motives, whether personal or national, are wholly unmixed, but this generous action was without direct historical precedent and in heartening contrast to pre-war American isolationism.

The plight of the refugees has been the concern of the United Nations, of great voluntary bodies such as the International Red Cross, the World Council of Churches (through its constituent Churches), the Society of Friends, the World Alliances both of Y.M.C.A. and Y.W.C.A., and of those particular nations into whose territory the hapless refugees have poured. Despite all such enterprise there still remains a seemingly irreducible minimum of many millions of refugees and expellees in Europe alone. To these must be added the Arab refugees who have resulted from the Arab-Israel conflict, and the uncounted numbers in Hong Kong, in North and South Korea, and in divided Vietnam. Nevertheless compassion has found practical expression, and through official and private agencies, millions of people have found a new start in a new country. It is a continuing responsibility.

Meanwhile the population of the world continues to increase with frightening rapidity and the birth-rate is higher in countries which can least bear the economic strain. In Asia the vast majority of people have a standard of subsistence which Westerners would regard as unendurable. Periods of famine or a national calamity can drag them quickly to starvation level. President Truman's famous Point Four and the Colombo Plan of the British Commonwealth of Nations have been addressed to this clamant need, and in Pakistan, India, and South East Asia, schemes of irrigation, modernized methods in agriculture, and assistance in stimulating native industries, have already brought notable advance. To help people to help themselves has ever been the worthiest form of charity, and the demand is for such assistance to be quickened in tempo and increased in volume.

The United Nations, through its Food and Agriculture Organization (F.A.O.), has steadily kept in view the interdependence of people and the necessity to regard the production and distribution of food in world terms. Nationalism in economics can be as dangerous as nationalism in politics. If when people sit down at a table the common rules of courtesy are disregarded and each grabs what he can get, then the weakest will have too little and the strongest will have too much. For far too long the tenor of Adam Smith's *Wealth of Nations* has been accepted, and commerce has been implicitly divorced from ethics. It has not only been assumed that you buy in the cheapest and sell in the dearest market, but that a country adjusts its tariffs and quotas to suit its own convenience and advance its own prosperity. It has been taken for granted a Government will so control the outflow and inflow of goods that its own traders are advantaged though the whole world suffer.

Even from a strictly economic point of view this has come under searching criticism. It can scarcely help the traders in one's own country if competitors are faced by high barriers and so are unable to trade. It is no help to the rich man to become richer still if his customers find it impossible or unprofitable to deal with him. On this elementary level, apart from any discussion of morality, it is an international, and not a rigidly national outlook on trade which is ultimately to the common advantage.

It was Lord Boyd Orr who drew most trenchantly the absurdity and wrongfulness of a situation in which, through maldistribution of the world's resources, there was a surplus in some countries and a shortage in others. Consider an essential commodity such as wheat. Often in certain States of America millions of bushels of wheat are left over, even when at lowest prices the last customer has been served. In countries such as India, there is on the other hand always the possibility of famine conditions when unnumbered people may starve. Lord Boyd Orr wanted to know whether, through the F.A.O. or a similar international body, the surplus of one area would be available for the desperate need of another.

The objector can postulate a thousand difficulties, economic, social, and even psychological in character. None however is insuperable if the will to assist be present. It is vision that is lacking, not technicians. Let men be convinced that it ought to be done, and the ingenuity of man will find a way. The challenge of Communism is for free nations so to organize their own resources that the needs of each are met out of the abundance of all.

In one of his books, Arnold Toynbee speaks of the immense stimulus Communism has given to political thinking. It was because Europe was so slow to learn the lessons of the Franco-Prussian War that Germany was allowed to become overwhelmingly strong and aggressive in the twentieth century and the first World War became inevitable. Even after that holocaust, nations slipped very easily back into old grooves of thought. The League of Nations was a collection of Great Powers using it as a parade ground, and refusing to abate one jot or tittle of their nationalist pretensions in the interests of the common good. When Japan in Manchukuo, Mussolini in Abyssinia, and Hitler in the Rhineland, found that the League of Nations was either powerless or unwilling to intervene, their aggressiveness was open and defiant. The situation was bedevilled because America had left President Wilson to his Fourteen Points and retreated in a certain sullen isolationism. In such circumstances a second World War could not be indefinitely delayed.

With the concluding stages of that war, it became obvious that Soviet Russia, despite its war wounds, was the new world Power capable of talking on equal terms with the United States and the British Commonwealth. Despite President Roosevelt's confidence in Stalin during the Yalta Conference, it quickly became apparent that in the post-war world Soviet Russia was not going 'to play ball'. Molotov became famous for his 'no' and Stalin for what in George Orwell's term was 'doublethink'. However soothingly he might speak, he followed a path of calculated aggression without the need for war.

In the Balkan countries, as in East Germany and Poland, it was a policy yielding quick dividends. On the long view however, its wisdom is not so apparent. Toynbee used the metaphor of the tank in which fish swim sluggishly to and fro until the larger truculent fish is put in and the mood changes from torpor to unwonted activity. The psychologists speak of action provoking re-action, and of an offensive attitude creating a defensive one. Under the pressure of danger, the free nations began quickly to learn the lessons of past history. The stimulus provided by Russian ambitions prevented the exhausted nations of the West from sinking back into accustomed alliances and counter alliances. In a single decade astonishing political advances were made.

Within the larger framework of the United Nations, statesmen secured, through the Paris Agreement of 1954, a closer integration of Western Europe than history had recorded since the break-up of the Holy Roman Empire. More extraordinary still, the Franco-German agreement on the Ruhr hastened the closing of an age-long break between the two countries. The coming of France and Western Germany into the West European Union will not by itself dispel old fears and animosities, but it accelerates the pace of mutual understanding and of eventual reconciliation. A consummation that only seemed possible in a distant future has been miraculously foreshortened.

Equally significant has been the development of the North Atlantic Treaty Organization (NATO), because it gives both Great Britain and the United States a continuing and vital part to play in the defence of Europe. The generous and imaginative statesmanship which gave sovereign status to India, Pakistan, Burma, and Ceylon, would have pleased Edmund Burke. He argued that 'magnanimity in politics is not seldom the truest wisdom; and a great empire and little minds go ill together'. The nations which comprise the British Commonwealth may have their many, and at times their serious differences. Nevertheless there is a real basis of unity, and together they form the largest single bloc of peoples in the world. Already the Commonwealth of Nations has exercised a salutory mediating influence in world affairs. Here is a meeting ground in which every continent in the world is represented. It is not just a forum for diverse approaches to common problems, but in its potential strength, an immense deterrent to the would-be aggressor.

Despite intense provocation, peace has been precariously maintained. There have been wars, some as costly and terrible as those in Korea and Vietnam, but the conflagration has been localized. The cold war has kept mankind in suspense, but total war has not overwhelmed us. In large measure this has happened because of the political response to the challenge of Communism. The best preservatives of peace have been the United Nations and its international agencies; the British Commonwealth of Nations, and the Western European organizations. Any coming together of free people within bonds of culture, commerce, social intercourse, and common security is justifiable so long as such an alliance has no aggressive intention. Two men who shake fists at each other may sooner or later come to blows. Two opposed blocs of nations who arm themselves to the teeth and then indulge in recrimination and provocative action may find themselves at war. The meeting with Russian and Chinese Communists; at whatever level and in whatever form, has always the ultimate objective of dispelling suspicion, removing causes of friction, and promoting the cause of international understanding and good will. It is saying in effect that existing alliances can be made larger still if the Communist bloc is prepared to enter. This may seem a more tortuous and laboured process than the simple expedient of world government but Utopianism is always suspect in political arrangements. There is no short cut to an earthly blessedness. The forelock of time must of course be grasped but only within the sequences of history. Seize the chances that are thrown up and larger opportunities offer themselves.

Where is the specifically Christian insight in this commendation of ever-widening, non-aggressive alliances? The very positing of the question suggests that the Christian directive cuts across temporal processes like lightning across the murky sky, that the Epistle to the Thessalonians is to be preferred in its reading of history to the Gospel of St John, and the catastrophic view of divine intervention to be preferred always to the Holy Spirit's working in history. This is a false dilemma, because it predicates an unreal choice of alternatives. Within history is both crisis and growth. To deny that there may be anything Christians can accept in post-war political developments is to deny the pressure of events which, rightly understood, is the hand of God in history; it is to reject the New Testament teaching that the Spirit of God is operative in the events of history and that He will teach if we are ready to be taught. What can and must be asserted is that the Christian subjects all historical processes to the searchlight of the Christian Gospel; he evaluates them in the light of Christian standards. To do that in the existential present is to recognize that the Communist challenge has been only partly met.

The Christian idea of alliance is not partial but total. There can be no stopping place until all peoples have a politically organized basis of agreement. The form of that agreement will unfold itself as men are responsive to the call of God in the events of time. But through the United Nations and the smaller alliances within it there must be the steady working of man towards an all-inclusive alliance. The necessary goal of mankind is the world society in which the various nations bring their particular gifts to a common treasury. The term 'peaceful co-existence' is in common currency and obviously the two halves of the world must exist together unless both are to die. Nevertheless this is one world, and co-existence at best is only a temporary halting place on the road to the common-sense goal of living as one family. Nor must one ever despair because 'the Communist goal is world domination'. The different ideologies of Communist countries make the task harder but in no whit abate its necessity.

Secondly, Christian insight can never approve the spectacle of great nations fully furnished with weapons of mass destruction. Mussolini offered olive branches hanging from the ends of four million bayonets. That, however, is no natural resting place for emblems of peace, as Mussolini discovered to his own cost. Olive branches come from olive-trees. This truth is being slowly apprehended by nations, not through inner illumination, but through bitter experience. On both sides of the 'Iron Curtain' there is, in words at least, the recognition that armaments must be scaled down to police force size, that all forms of atomic weapons must be abolished, and that further experimental tests in nuclear fission must be discontinued. There remains a vast amount of technical spade work to be done if words are to be translated into deeds. Details of inspection and control are fraught with particular difficulties, but if the goal be sincerely accepted, then the path leading to it will be found. There can be no true easing of tension and no freeing of man's energies for the arts of peace, until disarmament is regarded not as a romantic dream, but an inescapable necessity. Let a real start be made, and the substantial reduction will seem like an actual weight lifted from the shoulders of man. The change in psychological attitudes will be dramatic. 'Nation shall not lift sword against nation, neither shall they learn war any more.' We can discern the signs of the weather. Are we yet chastened sufficiently to discern the signs of the times?

The meeting of the heads of the four Great Powers at Geneva in July 1955 marked a new attitude of confidence which psychologically is of the greatest importance. It was not so much that there was agreement on any specific issues, as that there was agreement on the basic fact that modern war is ruinous to any nations involved. The various steps which have followed since have not seemed a logical out-working of this will to peace. Like a distant summit to an eager climber, the goal can at one time seem near, and at another time appear to have receded indefinitely. Unqualified optimism or pessimism are both out of place. There is needed an adequate philosophy of world relationship, a realistic appraisal of the limitations and possibilities of human nature, and a dynamism to overcome every obstacle. These three essential requirements are met in the Christian Faith. The challenge of Communism is a challenge to the Christian West to make explicit in political terms what is implied in its Christian creed.

There remains the religious challenge of Communism. Despite the welcome *rapprochement* of East and West, and the perambulation of Soviet leaders, it is well not to allow a desire for understanding to obscure essential differences between the Communist and Christian ethic of the State, of society, and of the individual.

In recent years Russian Church dignitaries have paid official visits to other countries, and enheartening accounts have been given of the Church attendance and Christian allegiance of great numbers within the U.S.S.R. This could be said equally of the Baltic States, of Poland, of East Germany and of the Balkan countries. Such impressions, backed by unassailable figures, still do not make the slightest difference to official Communist doctrine. The Marxist-Leninist creed is uncompromisingly atheistic. In Philip Leon's phrase, it would maintain that 'we must be the creators of goodness and the begetters of God'. Marx declared that 'the omnipotence of God is nothing but the fantastic reflection of the impotence of people before nature and before the economic social relations created by themselves'. In his book *On Religion*, Lenin developed the idea farther and argued that 'fear created the gods'. He went on to say: 'All contemporary religions and Churches, all and every kind of religious organization, Marxism has always viewed as organs of bourgeois reaction, serving as a defence of exploitation and the doping of the Working Classes.'

If there is no God, then the State becomes an end in itself. It demands for Caesar the things which belong to God. Freedom granted to any voluntary organization, such as the Church, can only be within set limits. No criticism of the State can be permitted, for the State has taken the place of God. Once again, as under the ancient tyranny of Antiochus Epiphanes, the 'abomination of desolation' stands in the holy place. The Christian Gospel is a flat denial of this blasphemy. The Christian says to every temporal authority what Christ said to Pilate: 'Thou wouldst have no power (*exousia*, R.V. authority) against me, except it were given from above.' The State therefore can never be an end in itself, demanding the total obedience of man. In its functions and the discharge of its powers, it is answerable first to God, and then to the people whom it serves as God's vicegerent. 'We must obey God rather than men,' said the first Christians, and the same answer is always given when the State oversteps its natural authority. That is why the Christian Faith is always the antidote against tyranny. In John Wesley's words, it asserts a Divine Power to whom governments and individuals are alike responsible.

The Communist ethic of society can never be absolute, but is always opportunist. This follows logically from its repudiation of God. Let God go, and goodness goes. The idea of a moral order and absolute values depends upon the moral character of God. Without God, the only meaning in life is a meaning we impose upon it. Beauty, truth, and goodness have no independent objective validity. Paul's triad of faith, hope, and love likewise has no ultimate justification. There can be no moral imperatives! What we decide to be right or wrong is the product of trial and error in social behaviour over many centuries.

But in a totalitarian State it is intolerable to allow an individual to decide for himself what is socially valuable; the State has its own code of the permissible and unpermissible. This is an opportunist ethic grounded in expediency. In consequence the State decides what is right and what is wrong on the basis of good citizenship. If a man is valuable to the State because of the correctness of his views and actions, he is 'good' in the one sense that matters. If he is unorthodox in his views and not 'reliable' in his political conduct, he is a 'bad' man.

The matter goes deeper still. Since the State refuses to believe in a moral order and absolute values, it has no moral compunction in making an individual conform to the social pattern. To that end it can justify a technique of falsehood, misrepresentation, and deceit, should exigencies of State demand it. Similarly it can employ methods of 'forced labour', torture and 'liquidation' if they seem advisable.

Against this ethical relativism, the Christian Faith asserts that there is a moral order which we defy at our peril. Values cannot be kicked about like a football; they express God's eternal purpose for His children. In the keeping of them is life; in the defiance of them is death. The Christian believes that only by these moral sanctions can society remain vigorous and healthy. Speak by all means of the spread of education, the continued extension of public services, the rising standard of living, the new economic opportunities, and only the churlish non-Communist will grudge his applause. Yet in the end the tone and temper of society is judged by its philosophy—by the goal of its striving, by its definition of the good life, and by the postulates on which it rests.

There remains the Communist ethic of the individual in his essential status and function. All that Communist propaganda claims for the happiness and well-being of its members who are loyal may be accepted, and still it is true that without God an individual is less than a man. If we are part of the fertile spawn of nature, born in the heat of a summer sun and to die in the cool of a summer eve, we have no abiding significance. We strive, we love, we suffer, but in the end we are tossed into the dusty unremembering grave. The grandeur and dignity of man arise from nothing inherent. Call him the crown of creation, and he remains but a superior species of animal. His unique importance comes only because he is important to God. If he is made in God's image, if the spirit of man is the candle of the Lord, if he is one for whom Christ died, if he is created for eternal fellowship with the Father, then beware how you treat him. He is not just a member of the State to be assessed in terms of his usefulness. Sweat him, rob him, oppress him, exploit him, and you will answer for his blood at God's hands. It is not in the province of any State to judge the

G

degrees of men's importance and to write off those who are useless or inimical to its purpose. 'The soul of the shoeblack', said Carlyle, 'is infinite, and all the pastrycooks in Europe cannot feed him.' It is still not recognized sufficiently that in the Christian Faith alone there is the very charter of democracy and the final vindication of the common man.

The challenge of Communism to the Christian Faith is therefore the call to assert the Christian ethic for the State, Society, and the individual. Only as it is contrasted with a philosophy which maximizes the State and minimizes God will its rich adequacy become apparent. This is the groundwork of any fruitful social philosophy. It is a word by which men live and without which they surely die.

Section III

THE DEBATE ON SOCIETY

CHAPTER VIII

THE TENANTLESS HOUSE

IT is a law of the spiritual world that as man increases God decreases. Let man be enlarged beyond his proper proportions and God dwindles in stature. There is, of course, an end to the process. When man is a colossus who rises to the heavens, God sinks into nothingness. When man steps into the place of God, he must say his prayers to himself and trust in his own right arm for deliverance.

The nineteenth century had its famines, its pestilences, its wars, and its consequent anxieties. They seem small enough to us, but the view from the wings is vastly different from that on the stage, and the picture of nineteenth-century peace, prosperity, and progress can be overdrawn. Yet Macaulay had no doubt of present and continuing material benefits: 'The history of England', he wrote, 'is emphatically the history of progress.'[1] Similarly, Gladstone and Cobden had confidence that internal economy and external free trade spelt progress, the poets with their virile belief in man's spiritual prowess saw no limits to his advance, and scientists lined up behind Charles Darwin to assert the evolutionary thrust of life and the upward climb of man. The great mid-century monument to this complete belief in man was the Social Exhibition held at the Crystal Palace, London in 1851. Those at home and those who came from afar were at one in their pride at man's achievements and their lively hope of his dazzling future.

This optimism could be combined with belief in God. Is not Victorianism commonly regarded as an age of belief and moral earnestness? God is, and man shall be—so Robert Browning in *A Death in the Desert* declared. Progress is

> . . . *man's distinctive mark alone,*
> *Not God's, and not the beasts': God is, they are,*
> *Man partly is and wholly hopes to be.*

But God remains in this picture, He has a somewhat passive rôle; the eye is focused on his creature—'the diapason closing full in Man'. The traditionally, and the naturally, religious section of the population held to a belief in God. But 'the Lord thy God is a jealous God'; to lose the sense of awe and of utter dependence is to lose the sense of worship, and if God is not worshipped He is already lost.

[1] Essay on Sir J. Mackintosh's 'History of the Revolution' in *Critical & Historical Essays*.

The magnification of Man was only a first factor in the decline of true religion. By itself it would not have induced men to leave Churches and gather with Auguste Comte, W. K. Clifford and Frederic Harrison in the worship of humanity. But discoveries in science appeared to make God unnecessary and to make man sufficient in himself. Charles Darwin's *Origin of Species* (1859) only proved Archbishop Ussher to be wrong. The Archbishop had proved the date of Creation to be 4004 B.C.; at one time that figure had been given in the margin of the Authorized Version, and for many people it seemed to have the same sanction as Holy Writ. If it was wrong the Bible was wrong. Far more than a particular date was involved; any definite date presupposed a special once-for-all act of creation, and if there was no definite date the Bible was not to be trusted.

Within a year of Darwin's thunderbolt came an explosion in an ecclesiastical armoury. *Essays and Reviews* may seem mild enough today and its plea for freer critical inquiry has long since been granted. In its own day it led to violent censure and heresy-hunting. The brave, however, were not to be deterred. In 1862 Bishop Colenso aroused a fresh storm when he applied the critical method to his discussion of 'The Pentateuch and Joshua'. When Professor S. Davidson ten years later published his *Introduction to the Old Testament*, he suggested that there were legendary elements in the Old Testament narrative, and he was dismissed from his post. One could indeed compile a Roll of Heroes, which would include men like Cheyne and Driver in England, Robertson Smith and G. A. Smith in Scotland, Briggs and Harper and Toy in America.

This historical and literary criticism has proceeded so vigorously that in the late Professor Sanday's words it has become 'international and interconfessional'. Because of the patient and devoted work of scholars the chaff has been separated from the wheat, and the authority of the Bible has been vindicated afresh. At the time, however, such criticism seemed both dangerous and destructive. It caused many thoughtful inquirers not only to doubt the inspiration of the Scriptures as the word of God, but to be critical of the Christian Gospel. In a book which had a world-wide reputation, Mrs Humphrey Ward wrote of 'Robert Elsmere', who through his critical reading came to deny the divinity of Jesus Christ and attempted only to follow his example as the great leader, and there were undoubtedly many like him.

Many refused even that stopping-place. They took the biological theory of evolution and erected it into a system of faith. God was discarded with the Bible. As someone has said, 'theology went out by the door, and ideology came in by the window.'

In our own century the movement away from God has been strengthened in three main ways. Firstly, this has been the Century of Wars. War is so prodigal of human resources, so careless of the individual, and so wasteful of human life, that it underlines the more savage aspect of existence. Men rarely ask the ultimate questions when they are faced with the immediate facts of suffering, sorrow, and death. Even the wanton cruelty of man seems to them but a reflection of cosmic indifference. The bombs get bigger and better until finally an atom bomb is produced. Man dispenses life and death on an ever wider scale. Towns can be obliterated and in time whole countries. Why doesn't God speak? The mystery of life presses hard upon those who are caught in the tangled skein of modern war.

Secondly, there is the obliteration of familiar landmarks. War itself produces a vast dislocation of normal life. The father is separated from the family; the mother engages in some war-time occupation; little children are brought up in nursery schools or removed to 'safe areas', though even in the country there still remains the heightened emotional disturbing atmosphere in which they must be reared during the impressionable years of their life; the men on actual service must live an unnatural life separated from their families and subject to terrifying stresses and dangers. Even when hostilities cease there still remains the long and bitter aftermath of exhaustion. After a long period in which people have been taught that to kill the enemy is the only way to live oneself, it is impossible for them at once to develop the arts of peace. Quite apart from their own spiritual upheaval there is the long slow struggle back to physical and material normality. The way to recovery is hard because it extends still farther the need for restrictions and controls. Nor can people resume the old pattern of existence. New houses must be built and in the meantime the newly married must live with their 'in-laws' or fret in rented rooms. For long years after the two World Wars populations were mobile because of re-housing schemes. It is estimated that between 1918 and 1939 one third of the population of Great Britain changed its residence. Under such conditions, people in their restlessness can very quickly lose a faith knit up with an older, more settled, and more peaceful order of life. In his poem 'It's no use raising a shout', W. H. Auden expresses this mood of disillusionment falling upon hurrying people who have no fixed destination.

It wasn't always like this?
Perhaps it wasn't, but it is.
Put the car away; when life fails,
What's the good of going to Wales?
Here am I, here are you:
But what does it mean? What are we going to do?

Thirdly, modern man has an ever-increasing number of counter-
attractions for his spare time. The Christian man must exercise his
spirit if he is to live. These religious exercises of prayer, Bible reading,
and public worship demand time and a certain detachment of spirit.
Unhappily such things are scarce. Truly there is more leisure than
ever, but spare time is more greedily devoured. There is the speeding
up of communications by road, rail, sea, and air; we never 'continue
long in one stay'. There is the increase of mass-produced entertainment; the book, the magazine, the concert, the play, and the film have
to jostle for place with radio and television. There is the world of
organized sport, and those who use it to exploit the gambling habit.
Far more relevant than when he wrote them are Matthew Arnold's
words:

What shelter to grow ripe is ours,
What leisure to grow wise?

The average man has not weighed Christianity in the balance and
found it wanting; it has been crowded out of his time-table and therefore out of his thoughts. He is not an atheist, because that assumes a
considered attitude of mind; but God has ceased to matter to him, and,
therefore, for all practical purpose has ceased to exist.

But as Nietzsche realized, God cannot die without serious consequences. The decline in religious belief, reaching a peak in post-war
atheistic existentialism, has had marked effects on the individual, on
community life, and on the plane of international politics. Let a man
free himself from moral restraints, and instead of obligation there is
only inclination; a man need only please himself. For the exceptional
man this may not be injurious to himself or the community, but for
most men the road is perilous. Public opinion and accepted conventions may deter a man from criminal folly, but he may still be entirely
self-regarding in his behaviour.

The man who only pleases himself is a bad husband and father;
family life suffers. The man who in his employment only consults his
own interests and desires is a bad workman. His eye is fixed eagerly on
the clock and the pay packet; he asks too easily 'What do I get out of

this?' and too rarely 'What is rightly expected of me?' The man who gets what he can from the State and evades responsibility is a bad citizen. Society is only the individual writ large. Let there be a sufficient number of people who, having forgotten God, forget the 'oughts' and 'ought nots' of life, and society is sick indeed. Pursue the matter farther. Assume a world in which for great numbers God is not a glowing reality but a figure of speech, a world in which, because men lack moral convictions, they are at the mercy of mass suggestions, a world lacking cohesiveness because men acknowledge no common bond. In such a world there can only be check and countercheck in a vast game of chess. Peace may be preserved precariously because prudence dictates. But what safeguard is there against the upsurge of demonic forces? What hope is there of any true advance to world community?

It is in the answering of such questions as these that there has been the notice of God's absence and the demand for God's return. The mood is dramatically represented in a grim story in the Gospels. There was a man out of whom an unclean spirit was cast. The spirit passed through waterless places seeking rest, and when none was found he returned to discover a tenantless house. So he took seven spirits more evil than himself and the house was occupied. Thus did the last state of the man become worse than the first.

Modern man has cast out a spirit with a compound name. In it are found such words as want, poverty, disease, and squalor. He prides himself rightly on such an achievement. Half the world enjoys this better standard of living and the other half struggles towards it. So far, so very good. But God has not been considered necessary; the work and the credit have been given to man. Consequently there is a spiritual vacuum. There is no *corpus* of belief, no common source of spiritual refreshment, no accepted goal to set before the eyes of men. The other evil spirits find a house swept and garnished but without an occupier. They are therefore ready to assume 'squatting' rights.

There are not wanting responsible theologians to assert that this means the invasion of demonic forces—'the spiritual hosts of wickedness'. The Indian fakir may solemnly contemplate his own navel, but man cannot perpetually contemplate his own soul. He cannot be the object of his own worship. Unless God is in possession, the spirit of man can be violently seized for ultimately destructive ends.

This can be expressed in concrete terms. Everywhere we are confronted by lowered personal standards of behaviour. Honesty is a word that is beginning to have an old-fashioned ring and various euphemisms are used to express the appropriation of goods or money from public bodies or private persons. Chastity is a word which is similarly out of fashion. Surveys such as those of Rowntree and G. R. Lavers in Great Britain, and Dr Kinsey in America, have shown a widespread sexual promiscuity. In the statistical *Review of England and Wales* for the years 1935 to 1939 it was shown that nearly thirty per cent of all first-born children were conceived out of wedlock. The effects of war and its aftermath may easily have produced more startling and dismaying figures. There is a sharp increase of eroticism in popular daily and weekly papers. In his important book on *The Film*, Roger Manvell lists the twenty-two ingredients which make up cinema entertainment for the multitude. The first five factors he lists as:

(a) Handsome men getting their girls (with or without sophistication).

(b) Handsome girls getting their men (with or without sophistication).

(c) Handsome clothes and handsome surroundings (luxury).

(d) Absence of clothes from women and to a lesser degree from men (sex).

(e) Ambiguous situations involving sex issues.

He further discusses the themes which are implicit in most pictures. Amongst them are the beliefs that 'the full-time pursuit of women by unoccupied business men and rich young *roués* is normal' and that 'sex is probably the most important sensation in life'. The record ends with the judgement implicit in films that 'life is a lark if you have the facilities, poverty is an act of star-slumming, boy gets girl is the end of life's difficulties, divorce is as easy as knife, and riches are the reward of virtue'.

Music Hall and the Stage reflected the uninhibited approach to sexual matters. In Great Britain at least, 'nude' shows with blatantly suggestive titles seem a stock in trade. In many plays and novels, chastity before marriage and fidelity afterwards are no longer moral absolutes but somewhat old-fashioned conventions to be ignored or defied.

But these media of public entertainment are only windows into a people's mind. From one angle they may be contributory causes to sexual laxity, but from another they merely reflect the contemporary code of sexual conduct.

It may be true that the majority of people are not specially dishonest, immoral, untruthful, or anti-social in their leisure habits. It still remains evident that religious sanctions have largely gone and that the 'respectable' live on religious capital which has accrued from past generations. For them it has dwindled into the things that are done or not done. They are held shakily by a public opinion which in itself is changing and insecure. The net result is often a nebulous morality overlying a hard self-regarding approach to life. Small wonder that this philosophy gives no mental or spiritual satisfaction. The word 'frustration' is in popular use because it describes how people feel. Deeper than a surface boredom and disillusionment is an underlying anxiety. It is caused not only by the troubles of an insecure atomic age but by the lack of a spiritual anchorage.

Dr Rollo May, the New York psychiatrist, in his book *Man's Search for Himself*, speaks of the loneliness and anxiety of modern man and he finds the roots of his malady in the loss of values—the loss of the sense of self, the loss of a common language for personal communication, the loss of the understanding of nature, and the loss of the sense of tragedy. But surely all these losses are in the end expressions of one great loss—the loss of God Himself.

No State can deal adequately with social evils and social malaise through its scientific, educational, medical, or social agencies. These things derive fundamentally from a decline of belief in God, and of that moral order of living inseparably associated with belief in God. Recovery, therefore, can only come fully with the rediscovery of God and the moral basis of life.

When Dr C. S. Jung discussed in his book *Modern Man in Search of a Soul* the chaos and darkness modern man will discover in his own mind, he declared that 'in order to live the patient needs faith, hope, love, and insight'. In the elaboration of that argument, he said in the memorable words so often quoted: 'During the past thirty years people from all the civilized countries of the earth have consulted me. . . . Among all my patients in the second half of life there has not been one whose problem in the last resort was not that of finding a religious outlook on life. It is safe to say that every one of them fell ill because he had lost that which the living religions of every age have given to their followers, and none of them has been really healed who did not regain his religious outlook.'

It is because his opinion is now widely shared that out of the social confusion of the day one can speak of the new demand for God. In Him moral standards obtain validity, and by Him there is the dynamic to sustain them.

With deterioration in morals, there is also widespread industrial unrest. This springs often from justifiable causes. Much as strikes are to be deplored as a method of gaining one's ends, they may still on occasion be the only way of securing legitimate rights. But there is much industrial disturbance which has no such sanction. It arises from the willingness to turn public discomfort to private advantage. It is often dictated by purely personal or class ends, and without any reference to the general interest or the national economy.

Industrial countries have their machinery of negotiation and arbitration. Their leaders know enough of applied industrial psychology to speak of the need for joint consultation between management and men, and for agreement between the various sections in industry. They know that the further need is for a working understanding between Government, Trade Unions, Employers' Federations, and representatives of nationalized undertakings. All this talk, however, breaks down in any country on the hard facts of human nature. Selfishness, ignorance, and wilfulness can smash the best concerted scheme. Nothing works unless there is the willingness to make it work. There is a growing realization that the true roots of much unnecessary industrial unrest may be moral and not economic. Lack of discipline or interest in work, excessive absenteeism, undue attention to short hours and long pay packets, and quick readiness to strike whatever public suffering may be involved, are only symptoms of disbelief in God and His claim over the whole area of life. They spring from a mundane conviction that man, left to battle alone in a meaningless universe, must do the best he can for himself in work as well as in leisure hours. He must do this in association with those of his own class or union who seek the same advantages, and he must pursue his claims even if the community is held to ransom.

Such an attitude is not to be met only by appeals to reason, justice, or fair play. It is not to be met by repressive legislation or other forms of coercion. It is not to be satisfied even by proper administrative machinery for negotiation. Ultimately, since the root of the trouble is religious in character, revolving upon a lost God and a lost pattern of living, the remedy must also be in the world of religion. In industry, as in society, the nature of what Edmund Burke called our 'present discontents' demands the return of God.

There is finally the field of international discussion. The tenantless house certainly knows the menacing spirit of an imperious nationalism. All over the world the former Empires are disintegrating. Even native people not fitted as yet for the task of self-government are intoxicated by the example of others, and demand loudly the expulsion of the 'tyrant overlord' and the granting of complete independence. Even when there has been a long and faithful record of wise administration and training in the art of government, the demand is still, 'do not stay upon the order of your going—but go!' Gratitude may be dormant rather than dead, but the immediate eager cry is for complete freedom. This may have its perils when a country, seizing its right to independence too soon, is shaken by difficulties and divisions within, and by the pressure of hostile interests without. More perilous still in the contemporary world situation is the jostling of Great Powers who are armed with atomic weapons of unknown proportions, and who are liable at any time to find that the conflict of their separate interests in any part of the world is producing a war which will engulf all mankind.

The need for alliances of the like-minded within the framework of the United Nations and for constantly enlarging the area of agreement with the Communist nations has been fully recognized. But despite armed strength and friendly conferences, the fear of genocide still haunts the minds of men. Can demonic forces engaging the fears and hatreds of men be for ever leashed by goodwill, compromise, and discussion? Are alliances and counter alliances enough? Great nations are called Great Powers. The primary meaning is that they are materially and militarily powerful, and the secondary meaning is that the power if necessary will be used aggressively. On the basis of prudential calculation can one ever conceive such power being used to serve and not to dominate? If nations are only governed by a wise calculation of risks and a careful regard for their own interests, can one feel for ever secure from the terrors of war? Even if the more blithe can answer affirmatively, there is a second and more important question: If they are governed only by worldly-wise motives, can nations ever come together in any form of world community?

The plain reply must be that only a constructive philosophy of life, a *Weltanschauung* of spiritual depth, could shape the goal and nerve the endeavour to reach it. In a word, the force and fury of international cross-currents, and the need not only to escape from war but to create a world society, is forcing man back to religious first principles. Let the world be conceived as a cock-pit, and the cocks will fight. Let it be conceived as a market-place, and men will buy and sell as customer and trader. But let it be conceived as the place God has intended us to occupy as brethren together, and there is the hope that we shall live in it as members of the same family circle.

In his monumental *Study of History*, Arnold Toynbee recognizes that science is laying claim to the whole of the spiritual as well as of the material universe, and that God the Mathematician is fading right out into God the Vacuum. But he believes[2] there is another way to what he calls 'the sense of unity'. He quotes a sentence of Alexander: 'God is the common father of all men, but He makes the best ones peculiarly His own.' Then he proceeds: 'If this be authentic, it tells us that Alexander realized that the brotherhood of Man presupposes the fatherhood of God—a truth which involves the converse proposition that if the divine father of the human family is left out of the reckoning, there is no possibility of forging any alternative bond of purely human texture which will avail by itself to hold mankind together. The only society that is capable of embracing the whole of mankind is a superhuman *Civitas Dei;* and the conception of a society which embraces mankind and nothing but mankind is an academic chimera. The stoic Epictetus was as well aware of this supreme truth as the Christian Apostle Paul, but, whereas Epictetus stated the fact as a conclusion of philosophy, St Paul preached it as the gospel of a new revelation made by God to man through the life and death of Christ.'[3]

The first great longing is for a world at peace, but this depends upon the recognition of God's sovereignty. In the process of history men were brought through the stages of tribal organization to that of city States or petty kingdoms. Thence they reached the stage of independent nationhood. But with the growing complexity of national rivalries, increased communications, expanding trade, and economic competition, they passed to a stage of alliances in which an uneasy balance of power was maintained. Further scientific discovery and technological advance made the world one. Cycles of economic prosperity and depression involved the whole world. Even whilst nations were striving for their own particular place in the sun, science and economics were making it impossible for them to live apart.

In 1914 two great alliances of nations fought each other, and by 1918 it was obvious that the only alliance sufficiently large to be safe was an alliance of all the nations. The League of Nations was a just outcome of events. It was a logical necessity in the development of history. It was another step in the divine strategy.

But a further stage was still necessary. It had to be shown by the hard facts of bitter experience that a society of nations which was founded on the selfish aggressive instincts of mutually suspicious Powers could not hope to endure. It hastened to its inevitable break-

[2] op. cit., Vol. VI.   [3] Abridgement of Vols. I–VI, D.C. Somervill, pp. 495–6.

down in September 1939. But the failure of the organization does not mean the failure of the idea. The conception is imperishable. It merely needs a new setting.

If wars, ever more deadly, are not to be recurrent, we must break the vicious circle. We must not begin with ourselves; we must begin with God. However much we try to avoid past failures by a skilful refashioning of world organizations, if we hope by agreement and discussion alone to maintain peace, we are lost.

If a company of well-intentioned burglars met to discuss how mutually they might surrender the tools of their trade, what would be the inevitable result? Or to use a slightly more pleasant metaphor, if a number of highly civilized business-men met to discuss how they could drastically limit their profits in the interests of society, what would be the outcome of such a gathering? The plain fact is that if egocentric men, representing egocentric nations, meet with the best of intentions to discuss the common good, there will spring up again the demons of greed, self-interest, fear, pride, and the rest of the hellish brood, to frustrate their best endeavours. It is not just an axiom of theology, but of life, that natural man is unable to save himself.

We recognize that the social, industrial, and international turbulence which fills with violence the tenantless soul of man needs to be exorcized. But these furies can only be driven out by the true master of the house. Born out of the anguish of these days is the realization that God is necessary in His own world. By the pressure of events we know our own limitations. The house must have its true owner. There is a recovered sense of the need for God.

CHAPTER IX

THE RETURN OF ORDER

ONE sign of God's departure is the lapse into chaos. Miss Francesca Wilson's book, describing relief work in Europe in and between three wars, was aptly entitled *In the Margins of Chaos*. After the second World War the delicate mechanism of civilization was stretched to breaking-point. Early visitors to ruined cities and silent battle areas were appalled to the point of despair. One of the shrewdest and most sensitive, the late Henry Carter, said 'the heart of Europe is only faintly beating'.

Parallel with this material breakdown of ordered life was the atheistic existentialism which flourished in intellectual Continental circles during early post-war years. It was a philosophical expression of prevailing despair. But the post-war face of Europe had for much longer been a representation of the soul of western man. In his *Drama of Atheist Humanism*, Henri Lubac traced the ancestry of that soul to Auguste Comte, Ludwig Feuerbach, and Friedrich Nietzsche. In the process of losing God, the pattern of living was lost. If there is no God there is no absolute groundwork of existence. Plato's cave-dwellers are left with nothing but the darkness of the cave itself. The only way to save oneself from regarding a world thus devoid of meaning and purpose as a madhouse is to impose a meaning upon it. But will your idea of reason correspond with your neighbour's? Will the accepted social conventions of one country be approved by another? Will a giant clumsy hand knock the bricks over again on to the nursery floor? In a senseless world, are there sufficient 'enlightened' persons to knock sense into it, or will the lunatics triumph? Despite the defiance of the cultured humanists, a loss of God has meant confusion in the arts, a lack of belief in the unity and meaning of history, a raping of the good earth, a dangerous all-in scramble for prizes in industry, and a divorce of science from the wholeness of reality. In a word, the disappearance of God has spelt intellectual chaos.

It is therefore a welcome sign that over wide areas of life there is a return to order. This decade might well be called a decade of discovery. Julian Huxley, whose professional competence in the field of science is only matched by his complete amateurishness in theology, has recently delivered himself of a characteristic statement. He declares that the power of God is disappearing rapidly from the universe like 'the vanishing smile of a cosmic Cheshire cat'. It would be hard to find elsewhere so unsupported a statement coming at so inappropriate a moment. The dictum would be strongly supported by many during the past hundred years. Today it is interesting as a comment on Julian Huxley's philosophical furniture, but not as an observation on the contemporary tide of thought. It would be foolhardy to claim that a recovery of order means a recovery of God. But that is certainly the direction of the wind.

If the thesis of a return to order is to be well established, it must show that return in three main areas of thought. It must show it in the new approach to the earth itself, in the scientific description of the earth, and in the history of man's sojourn upon it.

In the last twenty years a number of authoritative books have indicated a revived interest in the science of the soil. This arose from the fact that in widely different countries of the world a similar process was turning fertile lands into deserts. The dust bowl of Arizona may stand as a symbol for what has happened in North and South America, in Africa, and in Australia, when the earth has been exploited by the greed of man. For the ordinary man the story has been told movingly in John Steinbeck's *Grapes of Wrath*.

With the decay of belief in God came the decline of respect for the earth. Since it was no longer God's world, it was everybody's world. Let the boldest therefore take their plunder. The natural defences of the earth were destroyed. Trees were ruthlessly cut down. There was no longer any defence against the wind nor any roots of trees and plants to hold together the humus. In the words of Paul B. Sears: 'Man has upset the balance under which wind and water were beneficial agents of construction, releasing them as twin demons.'[1] The washing away of the fertile top-soil, and the consequent inability of the land to absorb the water which falls, turns the earth to desert. At a time when the human family is rapidly increasing there is this unprecedented shrinking of available land. A growth of population and a wastage of the land on which men must live cannot continue indefinitely. Mass starvation is the inevitable end of that particular road.

The flashing of danger signals has led to reform. There has been the attempt to repair the defences and restore the balance of nature. Soil conservation is restoring lost acreage and preserving existing areas of fertility. Ritchie Calder, in his book *Man against the Desert*, has described what has been done, especially by desert research stations in the Sahara, North Africa, and the Middle East. But millions of

[1] *Deserts on the March*, p. 4.

H

acres are irrecoverably lost and more will continue to be lost until the
principles of ecology are known and applied. Ecology, however, is a
new study, and as much an art as a science. It is the investigation of
how to live harmoniously with animals and plants in the same world.
The word stems from the Greek οἶκος, a house, and intrinsically the
problem is that of how to share a house together to the common advantage. This means that what is needed is not to study a text-book of
agreed principles, but to learn of a new attitude to one's natural environment. This has been well expressed by Edward Hyams: 'If man
can think of himself as one of the materials of the new art (creative
ecology) as well as the artist, he may yet learn from his ancient contact
with the soil to live nobly and be at peace.'[2] If he is to do this, man
must no longer stand over against nature but in with it. He can no
longer afford to be the exploiter, ruthlessly raping the earth for the
sake of maximum profit in a minimum time; he must learn to play a
humbler, more patient, and more co-operative rôle. He must have
regard to the structure of the earth and the needs of the soil; he must
obey the laws of growth and live in accord with the rhythm of natural
life. No good farmer can dictate to the earth from the top of a machine;
he must be willing to bend his knees. Moreover, there must be mental
as well as physical genuflexion; the earth must be respected. Only so
will it yield its increase. For thousands of years in Great Britain, and
many parts of Western Europe, as well as in the Far East, the soil has
retained its fertility. This is due to the fact that man has not departed
from an attitude of understanding and respect. He has not forced it
beyond its natural capacity, because he has realized there are certain
laws relating to the soil which cannot be broken with impunity. Now
that man the exploiter has become man the victim, we are looking at
nature afresh, and this after all is the dictionary meaning of the word
respect. This new look at the earth is the recognition that confronted
with Order man must be orderly. In his address to the Soil Association of Great Britain in July 1955, Louis Bromfield, world-known
farmer and author, declared himself convinced that 'the laws of good
husbandry were as precise as mathematics, and that the function of
science was not to discover anything new but to find out the patterns
of nature which had existed since the beginning of time'. But the
moment you speak of respect and of orderliness you are on the road of
moral imperatives, and at the end of that road is God. Why is the
earth so fashioned that only as we accept its order can we find it fruitful? And why ought we to accept this fact? The answer is that if the

[2] *Soil and Civilization*, p. 292.

earth be fashioned by God there is an obligation to treat it in the way God proposes. Defiance spells disaster. William Vogt has not hesitated to speak of ecology as a game of chess in which the player on the other side is hidden. He argues that the unknown player is always fair, just, and patient. 'To a man who plays well the highest stakes are paid with overflowing generosity. The one who plays ill is checkmated without haste but without remorse.'[3]

In this new, rapidly developing science of ecology, we are content at the moment to know that there are rules to the game; the earth has order. But it surely cannot be too long before men recognize that order does not spring from an ultimate chaos, and that if there are rules there is a Mind which is responsible for them.

Science is the loose generic term we use to describe our knowledge of the earth. But we go seriously astray if we suppose it is the only knowledge we possess. It measures and describes, but in this world there is the immeasurable and the indescribable. Lord Acton regarded science as the 'co-ordination of a great mass of similar facts into the form of a generalization, a principle or a law, which will enable us to predict with certainty the recurrence of events under like conditions'. The definition is unwieldy, but it emphasizes the descriptive nature of scientific knowledge. Science therefore is never a complete guide to reality. It can provide data, but it cannot supply final explanations.

The interpretation of these data led men down the long centuries to discover in science a clue to the workings of God. They did not depend on science for the proofs of His existence, but for the mode of His operation. Until the middle of the nineteenth century there was no so-called conflict between science and religion. Individual inquirers, sceptical of Christian truth, were present in science as in other fields of thought, but the main body of scientists believed that their investigations would only deepen the knowledge of God and of His activity. It has been the particular merit of the research work of Canon C. E. Raven, distinguished equally in biology and theology, to show the close connexion between science and religion which was only severed by the Darwinian controversy. In his Gifford Lectures of 1953 on *Natural Religion and Christian Theology*, as well as in shorter works, he has spoken of those pioneers in science who were actuated in their studies by a strong Christian faith. Not less than Copernicus or Linnaeus, men like Robert Boyle, John Ray, Ralph Cudworth, and Isaac Newton were pioneers whose religious faith sustained their

[3] *Road to Survival*, p. 274.

scientific inquiry. Joseph Priestley was a Unitarian minister, Mendel an abbot, and Malthus was an Anglican priest.

With the publication of Charles Darwin's *Origin of Species* the long and fruitful alliance of science and religion was broken. Oh the pity of it! For in truth it need never have happened. The theory of evolution was by no means revolutionary. Professor Herbert Butterfield in his *Origins of Modern Science* has shown that by the end of the eighteenth century 'all the ingredients of Charles Darwin's theory had already been discovered save the idea of the struggle for existence. The work of Malthus and the economic writings of the industrial revolution were soon to supply what was needed here, and the development of geological study—the work of Lyell, for example —prepared the minds of men for the *Origin of Species* in 1859.'[4]

In any case the theory did not deny God's presence or power, but only denied the instantaneous act of creation so neatly timed and tabulated by Archbishop Ussher. The immediate cause of the conflict was the memorable duel of words between Huxley and Bishop Wilberforce. The honours went to Huxley, and it seemed to many that not a Bishop, but the Christian Faith, had been worsted. Some outstanding Christian leaders like Arthur Stanley, Charles Kingsley, and Benjamin Jowett rejoiced in this new light of God's method in creation, whilst distinguished scientists such as Clerk Maxwell continued unshaken in their Christian Faith. The majority, however, on each side reacted according to their prejudices. Christians trembled for the Ark of the Covenant and took refuge in an unintelligent obscurantism. It is a commonplace of psychology that a defensive attitude will throw the opponent into a mood of offensiveness. Science became confident to the point of belligerency. The more polite on both sides preserved their peace but maintained their doubts.

This intellectual climate was not, of course, confined to Great Britain. But it was here that the break between science and religion came most sharply, and it is therefore fitting that in this same country should have come the *rapprochement*. From one angle it might appear that certain works of massive thinkers produced the change. Amongst these, S. Alexander, C. Lloyd Morgan, A. N. Whitehead, and Arthur Eddington certainly have their place. Equally there were books of great theologians, such as John Oman's *The Natural and the Supernatural*, and William Temple's *Nature, Man and God*, which served to bridge the gulf. But were these writers creators or heralds of the change? It is at least arguable that they only interpreted the intellec-

[4] Page 209.

tual drift of the time. The somewhat shy and hesitant approach of each side has not been without certain minatory claps of thunder. During one decade, between the middle thirties and forties, it seemed as though neo-Calvinism might hold back any attempt at understanding. Since then, however, the pendulum has swung back, and a much modified Barthianism remains as a necessary *caveat* but not as a deterrent. There are still, of course, those unrepentant scientific humanists who cannot come to terms with a Faith they regard as a vanishing superstition. There still remain therefore 'alarums and excursions', but, as in Shakespeare's plays, these are mainly off-stage.

The main cause of the new relationship between religion and science is once more the return to order. In science, as in ecology, the stress is upon cosmos, not chaos. The beginnings of the new attitude are not to be found in writers, but in the decline of materialism and the discoveries of Einstein. In the nineteenth century, physicists believed that the final reality was matter, and matter was composed of solid indestructible simple lumps of material. If matter is the bedrock of reality, then T. H. Huxley was right when he spoke of thought as 'an expression of molecular changes in the matter of life'; the mind, in all its adventures of thought, is set in motion by material processes, and cannot be regarded as the chief actor in the drama of existence.

But apart from the Dodo, nothing is now more dead than this materialistic explanation of life. For the sake of convenience physicists today speak provisionally of atoms, protons, electrons, and neutrons. The atom is in itself a solar system of such electrical power that its splitting is not only of major scientific interest, but of direct political significance. Atomic electrical explosion has already blown up traditional ways of thinking, not only in physics but in the whole intellectual gamut of life. Matter, of course, could not be blown up, because it was never there. Reality is explained not by material substances, but by energy in ceaseless movement. Movement and energy, however, are immaterial terms. Now, as someone has said, mysticism is explained in scientific terms, and science in the terms of mysticism. The end of materialism in physics, and the materialistic philosophy built upon it, does not in itself mean the end of agnosticism and the dawn of an age of faith. One bears in mind Susan Stebbing's warning in her book *Philosophy and the Physicists*. 'Christian apologists', she said, 'have been so eager to wait upon the pronouncements of the physicists, so thankful to be assured that we put into Nature the laws we profess to discover, and finally, that the chairs we sit in are not solid.'[5]

[5] Page 212.

Nevertheless the road is left open! For many, this ceaseless energy turns the mind to Abt Vogler's interpretation of the power behind music:

But here is the finger of God, a flash of the will that can,
Existent behind all laws, that made them and, lo, they are!

With the decline of materialism came a final *coup de grâce* in 1905, when Einstein's first theory of relativity stirred afresh the minds of men. The old three-dimensional view of the universe disappeared in what Weyl described as a 'cataclysm'.[6] It is only given to the few either to understand Einstein's developed theory or to explain it. But the word relativity makes it sufficiently plain that man cannot regard the universe objectively in absolute detachment. In terms of motion, observer and the observed are relative to each other. Man is therefore saved both from megalomania and despair. He is neither God nor Robinson Crusoe. He lacks the objectivity of the one and the solitariness of the other. He stands in relation to other people and to his environment. This again does not mean that God has returned as King into the minds of men but it does mean that, in Paul's words, 'boasting is excluded'. There is no longer place for a scientific dogmatism. The old confident sweeping of the telescope across the heavens and the announcement that God isn't there has given place to a new humility. There is even a sense of the immense mystery of life, and this is a first cousin to awe, which in its turn is a necessary approach to God. 'If any one imagines that he knows something, he does not yet know as he ought to know.'[7]

The old determinism, so rigid that even God was excluded, began to crack not only because of Einstein, but because of the quantum theory of light associated with Planck, and because of Heisenberg's law of indeterminacy. This last principle has seemed to suggest to some that there is 'free will in the atom'. To draw such a conclusion is to over-play one's hand, but even so, the iron rigidity of natural laws can no longer be maintained. The uniformity of nature is a presupposition of believer and unbeliever alike. Rational investigation depends upon it. But scientific generalizations cannot be given a sacro-sanctity since they are constantly in process of change and modification. If we are to speak of a 'wave of sound', a 'lump in space time', 'light on the bend', we can no longer employ at the same time the language of an iron determinism. 'Be not over-ready', said Karl Barth, 'to baptize into the faith, all unshriven, the last daring hypo-

[6] *Space, Time and Matter.*   [7] 1 Corinthians 8², R.S.V.

thesis of science.' The breakdown of a closed system of cause and effect, without incidentally the need of a First cause, does not necessarily lead to Theism, but it does enlarge the boundaries of the mind and allow for creative purpose and design at the very heart of things. In the words of the late Dr C. E. M. Joad: 'Science in fact has cleared the boards of the universe for religion, but it has no contribution to make to the writing of the play.'[8]

The beginnings of this new stage in the relationship of science and religion have been discussed. But what precisely is the present mental climate? There is a new interest in the conception of a purposive order in life. We shall never pick up again Paley's discarded argument from design. It was too mechanical to do justice to the continuing activity of God. The analogy of the watchmaker and the watch sets out the intricate perfection of the watch's mechanism, but leaves God in the position of a Creator who is no longer active. He may still be transcendent, but He is not immanent. How can a God like that be of service to a poor overburdened sinner? Nevertheless that same argument can still be used if it is re-stated in vitalistic and teleological terms. In essence it asks the evolutionist, How did the world as he knows it come to be? How does he account for the form and colour and design of nature? How does he explain the adaptability of the creature to its environment and the consummate provision there is for its existence? Can order come from chaos? No amount of paint will produce a painting; no box of letters will form a book; no collection of musical notes will compose itself into a symphony. In every case a directive intelligence is needed.

In that most readable of all the Gifford Lectures, *The Human Situation*, the late Professor W. Macneile Dixon indicated a direction which many philosophical scientists have followed in their separate lines of inquiry. He has no doubt of the 'racks and thumb-screws of nature', but he also knew the germ cell that 'contains within itself the power to develop the eye, the ear, the will, the emotions, the thoughts that make a man'. He marvels at the earth's climate, at the endless miracle of the human eye, at the under-wing of a butterfly and the outspread tail of the peacock. 'The spider mocks the mind and the caterpillar or the cockroach terrify the imagination.'[9]

This particular line of inquiry has been filled out in many admirable books. Experts have discussed the marvel of trees and plants, the life of the ant and the bee, the extraordinary properties of water and

---

[8] *Guide to Modern Thought*, p. 138. (Pan Books edition, 1948.)
[9] op. cit., page 143.

air, the song of a bird and the flight of a bat. The words of Jesus about the loveliness of the wayside flower and the provision of the raven's food have had appropriate scientific corroboration. In the late A. E. Taylor's book, *Does God Exist?*, another twist has been given to the argument. The author is concerned with teleology—that is, the doctrine that developments are due to the purpose or design served by them. The Greek word τέλος means an end and so the dictionary defines teleology as 'the doctrine of final causes'. A. E. Taylor is not, however, concerned with *finis* or τέλος as the end of the history of men; he seeks it in 'those numerous insects who instinctively deposit their eggs on a particular kind of leaf which will supply suitable nourishment for the coming generation of grubs though the insects themselves will die before the eggs are hatched. . . . The adaptation is to a remoter future, and the advantage secured is to the benefit of the still unborn off-spring, not of the egg-depositing insect.'[10] He goes on to argue that the life of organic nature is pervaded throughout by forward-looking adaptation. This is true of man himself, who by self-intention adapts himself to future situations. The teleological thrust discernible in organic life argues a purpose, informing nature and human nature, which moves towards a final consummation. No one reading Fred Hoyle on astronomy, or Joseph Needham on biology, or Bertrand Russell on Western philosophy, would assume that these distinguished scientists concurred. But if one is content to think of a general movement rather than of separate individuals, the climate today is favourable for a better understanding between science and religion. Once you begin to speak dynamically of order and purpose in nature, then certain consequences follow. It is not possible for any scientist to begin his research unless he assumes that the universe is a unity, is orderly, and is intelligible. Without these three assumptions he would be engaged on a wild-goose chase. Why seek for patterns if none exist, or the understanding of process if Nature lacks rhyme or reason? Yet to assume that the place we live in is a uni-verse, orderly and intelligible, is to be driven on to the belief in a single, purposive, orderly intelligence. As C. A. Coulson has remarked: 'If God is to be found in science at all, it must be as an absolutely integral part of it. There [is] no hope for any scheme which [tries] to fit Him in between the gaps left over after science [has] first claimed its possessions.'[11] The agnostic scientist could not begin his work without believing in cosmos and not chaos. If, as Walter Lippmann somewhere remarked, a man declares the world is a machine, 'it is because he is satisfied with

<hr>

[10] op. cit., p. 48.   [11] *Science and Christian Belief*, p. 64.

the analogy and will go no farther'. Yet in very truth he need but take one further step.

The mind which presupposes this order in life provides within itself a further clue to the Mind behind created things. Psychology is still suspect as a science in many quarters. But there is little satisfaction in describing and measuring the universe unless you have belief in the validity of the instrument you employ. It is a fatal weakness in the Behaviourist position that if you assume the mind to be an epiphenomenon, a mere by-product of bodily processes, then you take away your own right to pass any judgement; for if the body and its stimuli to the mind are all-important, how can you depend upon the mental instrument by which you come to these conclusions?

But a greater danger than Behaviourism has been the tendency in psychology to sum men up in terms of their instincts and sentiments. Psychoanalysis, under the immense shadow of Sigmund Freud, has familiarized us with the idea that man's mind is like an iceberg; the upper part which we call the conscious is above the surface, but underneath it is that greater part of the mind which we call the Unconscious. Trouble arises from the subterranean depths. Under the thin veneer of the civilized mind, able to keep sentinel duty over its thoughts and words, lies the instincts of the wolf and tiger. 'Freud has overlooked the fact', said C. S. Jung, 'that man has never yet been able, single-handed, to hold his own against the powers of darkness, that is, of the Unconscious.'[12] When our spiritual defences are too thin, the mind can be swamped by wild irrational impulses which may bring disaster. The arts, including religion, are only compensations for the denial or suppression of instinctive activity. Thus Freud can describe art as a 'temporary refuge from the hardships of life'.

Adler would supplement and to some degree modify this Freudian conception of the mind by his stress on the individual's need to compensate himself for a sense of inferiority. This explains the drive for power, success, and wealth in community life. C. S. Jung adds his contribution of a race consciousness which we all inherit and which unconsciously can influence our actions.[13]

In seeking to understand the wonderful blossom which is the human psyche, psychologists have shown marvellous skill in the dissection of the petals, but where is the flower? Split the rainbow up into its component colours, and with all your analysis you have lost the rainbow. The felt need today is not to leave dissected man on the

[12] *Modern Man in Search of a Soul*, p. 277.
[13] ibid., Ch. 7, p. 438.

table of the analytical psychologists, but 'to see him steadily and to see him whole'. That is why in psychology today there is a return to order. Man is not just a bundle of instincts, complexes, and repressions. There is no life in such a psychological monstrosity.

We must deal with whole men. Accept the essential truth of what the great pioneers have to say, and there still remains man as the self-determining agent of his own rise or fall. But succumb to the temptation to look upon man as merely the sum of the parts which psychologists have analysed, and what is he then? His mind is largely determined by unconscious processes; there is no longer any true freedom of the will; the way is open to determinism. Man is not a free agent; why then praise him for a right action or blame him for wrongdoing? A yawning gulf opens in which all our theology and ethics are lost.

Against this extremism there has quite properly been a revolt, which in another aspect is a return to order, and therefore to sanity. We do not pick up the separate parts in the psychologists' laboratory and try to construct a man. We start with man as he is, and then strive to understand the elements in his mental make-up. The revolt from a determinist view of man has been in another aspect the revolt from a mechanistic view of mind. Just as we no longer regard the action of the brain as a by-product of bodily behaviour, so we no longer regard the mind as a by-product of cerebral processes within the cranium. It is true that there is an organic connexion between brain and mind. Let the brain be injured and the operations of the mind can be impeded. Operations on the brain can alter the whole personality. The matter needs no argument. Even so, the mind is not to be equated with the brain so that all is explained by the excitation of the brain cells. The analogy of the telephone exchange is still relevant: there is the incredible mechanism which receives and transmits its endless messages, but it does not compose those messages and address them to itself; there remains the operator who uses the exchange. The brain is the instrument of the mind.

This recovery of man's status is not just a reaction against psycho-analytical theories which, as Kenneth Walker argued, 'leaves the problems of human soul where it found them'.[14] It is also due to the outstanding contribution of Christian scholars from all the great communions. The stress of neo-Thomism has been on the rationality of man and Thomas Aquinas has been thrust forward again as a champion of man's capacity nobly to think and nobly to act. This true humanism is not only the title of one of Jacques Maritain's books but

[14] *Meaning and Purpose*, p. 78.

the theme of others. In his *Range of Reason,* his main argument is that 'the only way of regeneration for the human community is the rediscovery of the true image of man and a definite attempt towards a new Christian civilization'.[15] Christopher Dawson and Etienne Gilson are other Roman Catholic writers who have influenced public thinking in their development of the same thesis.

But it is the Orthodox theologian Nicholas Berdyaev and the Protestant Reinhold Niebuhr whose massive thinking has moulded modern thought. Their greater understanding of man's sinfulness and the saving work of grace has given them a deeper understanding of man's divided nature than is possible in the Roman version of Christian humanism. But they believe equally that man was made in the image of God, and they resolutely refuse to surrender man to a 'scientific psychology which is as powerless as sociology to defend man's dignity and discover the divine image in him'.[16] These words of Berdyaev are reinforced by his final plea in *The Destiny of Man:* 'Act as though you could hear the Divine call to participate through free and creative activity in the Divine work; cultivate in yourself a pure and original conscience, discipline your personality, struggle with evil in yourself and around you . . . to further a creative regeneration of the wicked.'[17]

When Reinhold Niebuhr delivered his Gifford Lectures, he chose the same theme and virtually the same title: *The Nature and the Destiny of Man.* In his discussion of classical, medieval, Renaissance, and post-Renaissance, views on man, he states starkly the nature of that modern 'demonism' which makes an absolute claim for something which is not absolute. Whether it is done in the name of Nature, Race, or a particular form of culture, the effects are the same. He argues for that possession by the Holy Spirit which will enable a man to escape from the poison of a self-possession which means self-centredness.

But the significant tendency in the return to mental order, the establishment of the empire of the mind, is to be found in the field of psychical research. The phenomena of spiritualism have long been subject to careful investigation, and after every allowance has been made for fraud on the one side and over-credulity on the other, a residuum of evidence is inexplicable on ordinary grounds. The work of such Societies as that of the University of London Council for Psychical Investigation reveals the fact of abnormal phenomena even though no generally accepted explanations are given.

[15] Page 193.   [16] *The Destiny of Man,* p. 93.   [17] ibid., p. 377.

The most important work in scientific appraisal of these mysterious workings of the mind is the series of experiments in Duke University carried out by Dr J. B. Rhine. As a result of these investigations conducted since 1930 under the severest tests, the extra-sensory perceptions of the mind have been established as its normal property. Psychical research under laboratory conditions has also been carried out by Mr Whately Carrington, Dr S. G. Soal, Dr H. Thouless, and Dr J. Hettinger. Paranormal inquiry is nowadays not only a wholly respectable pursuit for scientists, but one with exciting possibilities. Mr G. N. M. Tyrrell, in his *Personality of Man*, has surveyed 'activities beyond the threshold'. There must still be suspension of final judgement about automatic writing, poltergeister, and so-called communications from the dead, but they strengthen the belief in the wider reaches of the mind.

Perhaps the most important field in modern inquiry into the mind's potentialities is that of telepathy. Only a few years ago a paper read at one of the meetings of the British Association brought into public view the work of scientists over many years. This indeed is experience which the layman can verify without need of the specialist. We have long known that a person in one place can know substantially what is in the mind of another thousands of miles away. Illustrations abound of people, emotionally related, such as parent and child or husband and wife, knowing 'intuitively' of something happening to a loved one. Later a telegram has only confirmed what the mind had already received. Modern investigations have not been so much concerned with a telepathy in space, which cannot be denied; they have pursued the line of pre-cognition telepathy, by which a person is aware of images and ideas occurring at some future time in the mind of another. It may well be that the next decisive step in man's knowledge of his universe will be his increased knowledge of his own mind. The development in mental telepathy will be an adventure in jumping the barriers of space and time as man communicates with his fellow man. Even more, it will illuminate the whole nature and art of prayer; for prayer in one aspect is a telepathy rising above the space-time continuum in which man communicates on deepest levels with the mind of his Maker. Charles Wesley speaks a quickening word to modern ears:

Give me on Thee to wait,
Till I can all things do,
On Thee, almighty to create,
Almighty to renew.

There remains for consideration those gifts of men's minds which express themselves in colour, sound, and form. The return to order in the study of the mind is nowhere more emphasized than in the recognition that man is a moral agent, capable of knowing right from wrong and of making his own decisions. Walt Whitman compared men unfavourably with cows, because cows do not whine about their condition nor speak about their sins. But to know what he is missing is precisely man's chief glory. It is only one who knows of a lost state who can speak of a future blessedness; it is only one who 'looks before and after' who can 'pine for what is not'. The Freudian psyche suggests neither a stable man nor a stable universe. It is a fit companion to a mechanistic view of life in which even the mind is a prey to dark primeval urges and

> *Chaos umpire sits,*
> *And by decision more embroils the fray*
> *By which he reigns.*

The recovered sense of rationality, of extra-sensory perceptions, of moral judgements in the mind, leads directly to a moral being in a moral order who is answerable to a moral God. Francis Bacon said that God never wrought a miracle to convince atheism, because His ordinary works convince it. Amongst those works there is the mind of man able to appreciate beauty, to be obedient to truth, and to follow after goodness. If the greater cannot be produced by the less, and if the mind of man is the greatest product in this universe, how much greater must be the mind which produced it. Indeed the argument goes deeper still. If man at his highest is capable of intense love, how infinitely more must be the love of God. This sequence of thinking has our Lord's sanction:

> *If ye then being evil know how to give good gifts to your*
> *children, how much more will your heavenly Father give*
> *good things to them that ask Him.*

It was a wise saying of Eddington that if he were told a living organism had been produced in a laboratory he would still be unimpressed. Before he accepted it as being a man he would want to apply one crucial test. He would want to know whether this new creation had a hunger for truth. Only if the answer was in the affirmative would he believe it was a real man. It is because the mind is beyond the resources of a laboratory, because psychoanalysis has no final power of definition, because the mind is master and not servant of the body, that modern thinking on the mind encourages man to say with Bacon: 'I would rather believe all the fables in the legend, and the Talmud, and the Alcoran, than that this universal frame is without a mind.'

In a recent play, the hero was engaged, he said, not in a study of history, but of historians and the philosophy which determined their viewpoint. It is a study which might properly be a subject for research. Leopold von Ranke, the nineteenth-century German historian, strove to write without any bias. Historiography was to record the truth with scientific disinterestedness. None can doubt his importance and his immense influence on the writing of history during this last hundred years. But is such an ideal neatly attainable, and can a writer pursue it without having to forfeit much vigour and allowable interest from his narrative? Ranke himself confessed that he could not. In the preface to his *History of the Popes*, he said: 'An Italian or a Roman Catholic, would enter on the subject in a spirit very different from mine. By indulging in expressions of personal veneration, or perhaps, in the present state of opinion, of personal hatred, he would give to his work a peculiar, and no doubt more brilliant colouring.' Moreover, despite his studied disinterestedness, Ranke could not forswear his own North German Protestant background. Supposing one adopts the thesis of this school and says with the late Professor J. B. Bury, 'History is a science, no less and no more', has the discussion therefore ended? Indeed not, for two facts at least remain with which to open it again. The historian must be in some sense not student only but judge, and he must attempt to unify the seemingly intractable elements in the human history.

In his book *The Historian's Craft*, the late Marc Bloch tells stories of two great French historians. When Michelet was explaining the nature of his work to St Beuve, he said that if he had only taken political history into his narrative and neglected the diverse factors of religion, law, geography, art, and literature, the procedure would have been different. 'But', he added, 'a great vital movement was needed, because all these diverse elements gravitated together in the unity of the story.' The second story concerns de Coulanges, who, a generation later, asked his hearers in the Sorbonne: 'Supposing a hundred specialists had divided the past of France according to lot, do you think that in the end they would have written the history of France?' He answered the question himself by saying: 'I very much doubt it. At the very least they would miss the linkage of facts; now this linkage is itself an historical truth.'[18]

[18] op. cit., page 154.

Here then is a double claim. The historian must in some sense be a judge if he is to arrange and assess the evidence which with scientific impartiality he has gathered. No one doubts the rationalist bias of Gibbon, the Whig bias of Macaulay, the Erastian bias of Froude, the Tory bias of Oman, nor the fact that such bias gave life and colour to their narratives. The reader knows, however, that their judgements must be corrected, because they are concerned only with the relativities of persons and events. They are not looking beyond the flux of space and time. They are, however, both scientists and artists, both analysts and assessors, both scholars and witnesses. It is their attitude which one approves, and not of necessity their conclusions.

If the historian adopts this rôle in the interpretation, not of the particular but the general, not of historical periods but history as a whole, will he be less likely to err in his conclusions? No historian is *ipso facto* a philosopher or a theologian. Unlike H. A. L. Fisher, who could only recognize 'in the development of human destinies the play of the contingent and the unforeseen', there are those who, in Fisher's words, 'discern in history a plot, a rhythm, a predetermined pattern'. Nevertheless though they are persuaded of order in history because God invests it with meaning, and though they may speak freely of the moral bias of life which operates in historical events, they can only affirm the pattern. Once they dogmatize upon it they pass beyond their profession as historians and set up as theologians. This they may have a perfect right to do if their qualifications are so wide, but they must be judged then by other criteria.

The significant feature in modern historical study is not the particular conclusions of historians but the standpoint adopted by them. Lord Acton is once more coming into his own. The view he expressed in his inaugural lecture at Cambridge that 'history is the true demonstration of religion' summarizes his approach to historical study. Always for him the essence of history was ethical. He agreed with J. R. Froude that 'the world is built somehow on moral foundations: that in the long run it is well with the good; in the long run it is ill with the wicked.' It is over fifty years since he died and during that period a prevailing disbelief was reflected in historical criticism. Even those who fully recognized his greatness as a historian discounted his moral judgements. They preferred to read Oswald Spengler. Now the tide has returned. The Hulsean Lectures in the University of Cambridge for 1933–4 were concerned with *Christianity and the Nature of History*. Dr H. G. Wood even entitled one of his lectures: *The Guiding Hand of God in History*. For him 'the hope of progress is linked with trust in providence',[19] and history is 'a reiterated call to repentance'.[20]

The two names most associated with this return to order are A. J. Toynbee, and Herbert Butterfield, Professor of Modern History in the University of Cambridge. Arnold Toynbee's monumental work *Study of History* is not merely the record of the rise and fall of twenty-one civilizations but a judgement upon them. The important consideration is not in such generalizations as 'challenge and response', 'the golden mean', 'schism in the body and the soul', but in Toynbee's organic view of history and the moral judgements he bases upon it. In the human story he finds that after swordsmen, archaists, futurists, and philosophers had all failed, only the gods were left. 'And now, as we stand and gaze with our eyes fixed upon the farther shore, a single figure arises from the flood and straightway fills the whole horizon.' There is the Saviour 'and the pleasure of the Lord shall prosper in his land: he shall see of the travail of his soul and shall be satisfied'.

In a number of books on the general meaning of history considered organically, Professor Herbert Butterfield has rejected dogmatic moral judgements based on events in time. He is too fearful of the historian as judge and prefers him in the rôle of expert witness. For this reason he is critical of the Whiggish bias of Macaulay or even of Lord Acton. Nevertheless he is confident that history is susceptible of moral meaning. We dare not minister to our own self-righteousness, but we can see the consequences of private and social sins in history. Since history 'exists for the glory of God', men in time are always under judgement—a judgement to reward or condemnation. His argument is that belief in God gives greater elasticity of mind and rescues a man from too great subservience to intermediate principles, whether these are related to nationality, or ideology, or science. His conclusion strongly resembles that of Toynbee in its stress on Christ's uniqueness. 'Hold to Christ and for the rest be totally uncommitted.'[21]

The belief of this school of historians in the sovereignty of God, the universality of sinfulness, the solidarity of mankind and the rewards and punishments consequent upon a moral basis of life, are important data for the theologian. Taken together with similar movements in ecology, science, and psychology, the accumulated evidence indicates the unity, intelligibility, and moral purposiveness of life. But how can you make those three assumptions without the further assumption of a God who gives life unity, rationality, and moral structure? Must there

---

[19] *Christianity and the Nature of History*, p. 152.   [20] ibid., p. 142.
[21] *Christianity and History*, p. 146.

not be the one Mind, itself rational and moral, to make such a world and such men upon it? Theism may present its difficulties, but they are of gossamer-weight compared with the difficulty of explaining this cosmos on the basis of an endless number of accidents and coincidences.

The return to an idea of order in those branches of knowledge which concern the earth and its people is in effect a return to God. On this showing, the revival of interest in religion is not to be deduced from the success of evangelistic campaigns, because the mass of the people still remains unmoved. It is to be found rather in a rejection of that disbelief which bowed God out of His universe and allowed man to sit on His throne. We have discovered to our cost that God and the moral order of life go together. Rid yourself of God and you rid yourself of order: the world came accidentally; morals are a social convention; men and nations must fight it out in an amoral arena, and no mercy need be shown, for no Arbiter is present! Disbelief in God leads to anarchy in morals, opportunism in society, and a relentless struggle for power among the nations of the world. Disorder is King!

Return again to the concept of reason and order in life, and the revival in religion has begun. Past experience suggests that it will be a generation before the fullest effects of the present return to order are experienced, but the direction is right and the road is the King's highway. He that hath eyes to see—let him see.

CHAPTER X

UNFINISHED HIGHWAY

THE recovery of order is still partial and incomplete. 'Exit chaos, enter cosmos' does not mean that in every sphere of man's activity there will be the same regard for order and the same search for a basis of law. Yet there can be no resting-place for man's spirit until the harmony he has begun to discover is seen to dwell in every part of the world. The quest must be undertaken in the four principal spheres of human living. We are born into a family, and the first and always the most important early influence is that of our home. Then follows education and the long preparation for life spent in schools, colleges, and universities. Sooner or later we must work and fulfil the twofold aim of satisfaction to ourselves and benefit to the community. There remains finally the amount of time at our own disposal to use as we think fit. It is significant that already some speak of the 'problem' of leisure and not of its opportunity.

THE FAMILY

Firstly, then, it is necessary to seek a proper basis of authority in family life. If order be absent there, the members can neither be good neighbours in their community nor good citizens in their country. Where is the principle of authority to be found? In different ages and different civilizations the matriarchate was the strong unifying force in family life. But the patriarchal principle has for many reasons been the tougher, and the Roman paterfamilias has had a long line of succession. In Oliver Goldsmith's play *The Good-natured Gentleman*, Leontine says to his father, 'An only son can expect some indulgence,' and Croaker replies: 'An only father can expect some obedience.' In the last century certainly the father was the undisputed head of the family. When the father of Elizabeth Barrett Browning spoke to his many sons they clicked their heels and said 'Sir'.

There were many reasons for this position of authority. The wife had neither time nor opportunity for outside work. Her place was in the nursery and the kitchen. The father was, in popular phrase, the family 'bread-winner'. It is true that children at an early age were expected to find an occupation and earn money. Even so, the money went to the father. He was the guardian and dispenser of the family income. Then again, his social position was superior to that of the woman. The legal status of a woman is succintly described in Blackstone's *Commentaries:* 'Upon marriage her legal existence was suspended, and incorporated and consolidated into that of the husband.' She had no freedom over the disposition of her own property. She had no power to vote. With certain exceptions, no career was open to her. The condition prevailing in England was not widely different from that in other parts of the civilized world. Finally, fatherhood had a certain distinctive religious aura. Until the outbreak of the Darwinian controversy and the beginnings of higher criticism, the generality of people accepted a literal view of the Bible. The Old Testament had equal importance with the New Testament. People therefore had sympathetic acquaintance with a patriarchal society. Was not God 'the God of Abraham and Isaac and Jacob'? The impression was deepened in the New Testament. Was He not also 'the Father of our Lord Jesus Christ, of whom the whole family in heaven and earth is named'? There seemed biblical sanction for the authority of the male parent.

In time, owing to the pressure of many circumstances, the power of the father diminished, and no fresh basis of authority was found. This led to family distress and confusion, to the great hurt of society. The disintegration of the father's authority came first with the change in his economic status. With the passing of the years, and in the quickened tempo of two World Wars, women began to earn their own living. Today it would seem that the Christian Ministry is the last stronghold of the male, and even that position has been breached by one or two great Christian Communions. A woman often maintains her job after marriage. Children continue their studies for a longer period, and when they do begin to earn, they no longer pass over their money unquestioningly to their father. The distribution of the family income is much more a matter of general agreement.

Secondly, the social status of the father has altered with the growing importance of the mother. The nineteenth century was one of individualism. In one aspect it was the struggle for freedom, and not least the freedom of woman from several disabilities. In course of time she secured the right to vote, the full disposal of her own property and economic independence. Sex equality is no longer an aspiration but an actuality.

Lastly, there was first the questioning and then the denial of the religious sanctions for a father's authority. A more dynamic view of the inspiration of the Bible caused men to realize that the patriarchal system was an ancient and outworn system of society. The fact that in Christ there is neither male nor female had a much keener contemporary ring. Unhappily a growing number of people did not turn to the Bible at all. Two World Wars hastened a process of unbelief. To compensate himself for the loss of God man turned with greater zest to the increasing number of pleasant distractions that his own technical ingenuity was providing. The very word 'authority' had an odd sound. It kept company with similar words such as discipline, order, and obedience. All belonged to a world of 'ought' and 'ought not', a world of moral values and obligations. This was not the world in which the many felt happy. It ran contrary to their desires and inclinations. It clashed with the hedonism of 'I want' and 'I do not want'. It was stuffy, old-fashioned, and inhibiting. It had no place in a brave new world. Away with it! When the second war was over the divorce rate in many countries reached record figures. Beyond that stretched the number of annulments and legal separations. People even spoke of the collapse of the family. They forgot its toughness; but there was certainly a collapse of the old standards. No longer was it thought necessary to remain chaste before marriage. It became questionable whether fidelity after marriage was demanded. The father's authority had gone, and with it the old stability and cohesion. Children who had been separated from their fathers by the weary years of war, and who, divorced from normal family life, had been subject to abnormal stress, were the 'problem children' who could so easily become delinquent and at enmity with society. All countries had their own equivalent of the 'thug', the 'tough', the 'rowdy', and the 'cosh boy'. Family life was in the melting pot.

Slowly and painfully there has been a return to order, but progress is still slow, because there is no agreement about the true basis of authority and its sanctions. There are three possible attitudes to a new order in family life. One attitude is the nostalgic yearning for the past, the attitude of those who are always reminding children of what parents used to expect, and of the good old days when their grandparents were young. This is both unrealistic and harmful. It can provoke both boredom and resentment, and these can stimulate a reaction against the past and all its ways.

Then there is the pagan attitude of sophisticated opportunism. The family is regarded in the light of personal convenience. It is blandly assumed, since lip service must be paid to the awakened desire of order, that such conduct accepted by all the members of the family will make for good-natured and tolerant agreement. The sex instinct is divorced from its social function and is not integrated into the structure of the family. It is used in the service of private lust without any social reference. Such 'enlightenment' not only breaks family ties and mocks at community obligations; it keeps the family on the level of the farmyard. No order is to be found on the basis of 'live and let live' when each lives to himself.

The third attitude involves the re-establishment of authority. But order is not now achieved by establishing the authority of the father or the mother or the child—(there is no tyranny like the tyranny of children). Authority must rest upon the family as an organic whole. It must be based on father, mother, child, as a living society. This is in accord with the philosophy of the age. We accept the postulates of social democracy in which there is not the self-assertion of the different members of the family but their co-operation in the interests of all. It is the true biblical view of marriage, which is likened in the New Testament to the mystical union that is between Christ and His Church.

How can this authority be secured? What are the necessary steps to a recovery of order? External aids must be used. In the Pauline view of the State, it is affirmed that whilst the State cannot produce the good life, it can make it possible. We now see that it can do this by coming to the help of the family when it is most needed. That is why, for the effective functioning of family life, there must be some form of social insurance. Help must be given at times of sickness, child-birth, old-age, and death. A vital task of the State is, directly or in-directly, to provide accommodation for married couples. An urgent need is for houses. It is intolerable that so many young married people have to live for years with their 'in-laws'.

There must be inner as well as outer resources. An order which depends upon the recognition of each other's particular place within the family circle can only be maintained by an adequate philosophy. There is honour due to parents, and love due to all. This can only rest on a reciprocity of giving and receiving. The danger is not that the parents may expect too much from each other but that they may expect too little. If the authority of the family lies not in any separate member but in its wholeness, then the husband must expect every-thing from the wife, as she must from the husband; and both must expect from their children and their children from them.

It is not special pleading to argue that this waiting upon each other is nourished by a common waiting upon God. Daniel Niles has said that many are willing to serve God but not to be served by God. They are not ready for God to wait upon them. Yet the whole genius of the Christian Faith lies in the symbol of empty and outstretched hands.

It is only by God's grace that the family can recover its order and authority, for only then can the family be replenished in its peace and power and joy. A family so replenished is the salt of the earth, for it is the preservative of society.

EDUCATION

If order must be reimposed in family life, then equally it must be sought in education. The second question to be asked of society follows hard upon the first. After asking what education is for, we must immediately inquire whither it is going. Education is the means whereby we can best enjoy the good life. But does our educational system fit us to secure that end? Whither does education lead today?

The question takes us farther back than a discussion of the necessity or non-necessity of public and private schools, of the necessary or exaggerated emphasis on technical education, and of the advantages or disadvantages of the present examination system. It takes us back to fundamentals. We must start from the postulates that education must secure an integration of knowledge, an increased capacity for wonder, and the mood of reverence.

One disastrous consequence following the breakdown of the medieval solidarity in religion and politics was the disintegration of the medieval synthesis of thought. In that accepted philosophy of life even economics was a branch of ethics, and warfare was discussed in terms of the just and unjust. The year was not a secular measurement of time, but the Christian Year, in which the drama of man's redemption was annually observed. This empire of thought was rudely shattered when man's emergence threatened God's sovereignty. Gradually the former unity gave way to a departmentalizing of thought. Machiavelli, in his *Il Principe*, broke with the idea that government was subordinated to religious ends, and made religion an instrument of government. Politics was not an aid to the good life; it was the good life itself. He laughed at the idea of politics for God's sake and asserted the necessity of politics for its own sake. The science of politics was therefore autonomous and must tolerate no outside dictation. Sir Thomas More drew a picture of *Utopia* in which the people's religion was to be distinguished from politics. Thomas Hobbes in the middle of the seventeenth century drew in his *Leviathan* the picture of an absolutist rule from which all considerations of religion had been excluded. It has been said that Cromwell's foreign policy was the last occasion in English history when religion exercised a major influence. Common to political philosophers of the eighteenth century, whether in Europe, England, or America, was the idea that politics has its own rules and must not subserve a larger system of thought. Even those philosophers who spoke of man's natural rights never spoke of them as derived from God, but from a state of nature and the contract into society. Political autonomy has been achieved.

It is perhaps not too fanciful to trace the ancestry of our modern 'scientific attitude' to life to the founding of the Royal Society. Francis Bacon had declared the undreamt possibilities of applied science, but when the Royal Society brought men of like scientific interests together there was a passion for experimentation. It was harnessed to the service of transport, communication, agriculture, and industry. These men were commonly men of faith but their minds had separate compartments. They were content to pursue their researches without supernatural reference. Charles Wesley might write a hymn about the Lisbon earthquake (1763) drawing highly moral conclusions from the disaster, but the truly significant fact is that for the first time the explanation given and accepted was scientific. There was not talk of an 'Act of God', but only of a convulsion of nature explicable in natural terms. In that sense the earthquake marks a turning point in modern history. Theology gave place to science, and the right to give a total scientific explanation was accepted.

The real significance of the Darwinian controversy is that it marked the final assertion of science to make its own observations on the universe without reference to natural or revealed religion. The conflict soon became a truce which was akin to a genteel cold war. Scientists were elaborately polite in outward reference whilst Christians kept warily on the defensive. But neither side believed it could receive light or help from the other. Scientists were prone to believe that they could give a total explanation of life, and delivered their judgements without any painstaking intellectual sifting of the Christian case. Christians suspected that scientists who began by discrediting the Bible might end by discrediting the Faith. The whole root of the trouble lay in the fact that science had asserted its complete autonomy, and could not be brought to recognize that its insight, though valid, was only partial.

The fight for independence within their own spheres won by politics and science was extended to economics. The tragedy of the Industrial Revolution is that it was not disciplined by any religious philosophy and moral standards. Contemporary writers such as Adam Smith spoke of 'economic man' as intelligent in the pursuit of his own interest. He always buys in the cheapest and sells in the dearest market. He is not to be moved by considerations of morality but only his own advantage. The greatest happiness of the greatest number, according to the dominant utilitarian school, would be secured by giving free rein to individual initiative. This reduced life to the level of an arena, in which the race went to the swiftest, the fight to the strongest, and the prize to the most unscrupulous. The conditions were excellent for the possessors of wealth, rank, and privilege; but what chance had the sick, the aged, the destitute, and the infirm? For that matter, what chance had the child or the woman? This was the age of the child chimney-sweeper, the woman in the coal mine, and that savage treatment of the pauper which was only exceeded by the official behaviour towards the insane. The well-meaning moral safeguards which Christian social reformers set up to deflect into right channels the course of Industrialism were swept away by the raging torrent of Individualism. Economics was no longer under the control of religion; it existed in its own laws and justified its own autonomy. Much of that fury has spent itself. The 'Manchester School' of economic theory belongs only to history; the 'laws' of economics are no longer regarded as immutable; the idea that self-interest conduces to the general interest has long since been abandoned. Nevertheless the belief that ethics has no place in business is slow in dying. The strangest Christian challenge to a typically modern man is that he has a moral responsibility both in the way he earns his money and the way he spends it. Economics has successfully achieved autonomy and 'business still is business'.

Once, however, you begin to departmentalize life, where are you going to stop? If politics, science, and economics, can be divorced from religious considerations, why should not the world of culture? Poetry, art, music, and literature must go their several ways, submitting to no discipline that is not self-imposed. 'Art for art's sake' is a slogan of general application. If one complains of verse without appreciable sense, art without apparent meaning, music without recognizable form, writing that loses itself in a waste of words, the defendants refuse to accept such canons of judgement. They only demand that the various branches of culture be true to themselves, obeying 'an inner rhythm'. It is the assertion of cultural autonomy: 'Hands off the Arts.'

This process has gone so far that now, as we all know, we live in an age of specialization. Our dilemma is that specialists are so specialized they do not know what other specialists are thinking and doing. Autonomy has gone so far that in the world of the mind there are innumerable cultural boundaries which few seem able to pass. Truth, therefore, has been shattered into fragments and no one seems able to assemble the bits.

One window into the present state of affairs is shown by our educational theory and practice. The child has his time-table of different subjects to be taken at different hours of the day. He wanders from one classroom to another. Having taken one period of mathematics, he now takes history, and then geography, and finishes the morning in the physics laboratory. During the course of the week he may also have studies in one or more languages, literature, chemistry, and an odd hour of scripture. The curriculum and procedure may differ according to place and circumstance, but the method of education in England as well as in other countries remains the same. But this sort of teaching only perpetuates within the school the confused unrelatedness of knowledge which exists in the world outside. There is no integration of knowledge, no agreed systematic attempt to recognize all branches of learning as part of the common search after truth.

Yet to speak truly, all branches of mathematics and science constitute one approach to reality as the arts mark another. They all contribute to a heightened awareness of the world we live in and the creatures that we are. No child, therefore, leaving one subject for instruction in another, ought to feel he is proceeding to something entirely different. The end of education ought to be to reveal the relatedness of all subjects, since all light up the one all-embracing truth about the world and our lives within it. For this reason, the periods devoted to the Bible and instruction in the Christian Faith are not extra subjects for study. Here, if at all, is the clue to the whole; here can be found the unifying thread tying together all the subjects in the curriculum and giving them meaning and coherence. For this same reason, when a school gathers together for worship there is a supreme opportunity to realize that knowledge, like peace, is one and indivisible. A basis for order, in studies otherwise so different, is afforded in the Christian interpretation of God and the nature of His world. With this true centre of integration, a student can know that the study of mathematics as much as that of history, the lessons in poetry as much as those in geography, may be to the greater glory of God and the fuller appreciation of His universe. Lacking this clue, we wander in a maze, like the characters in Jerome K. Jerome's book,[1] without ever reaching the centre. The scientist and the mathematician, like the philosopher and the theologian, assume the unity and

[1] *Three Men in a Boat.*

intelligibility of the world. In practice, however, we deny that insight when we give separate subjects a separate autonomy.

There are not many glories, but one, and

> *'Tis ye, 'tis your estrangèd faces,*
> *That miss the many-splendoured thing.*

I would join together a saying of Irenaeus and the last sentences in John Oman's *Vision and Authority*. 'The glory of God', said Irenaeus, 'is a living man; and the life of man is the vision of God.' But this *summum bonum* is not the preserve of the mystics. Said John Oman: 'The demand which should ever ring more loudly in our ears is to inquire more earnestly, more humbly, more patiently, more utterly in the spirit of love and with a more exclusive regard to the interests of truth. So shall we follow Him who is True and see the glory of the Kingdom which is Love.'[2]

Secondly, order in education means an increased capacity for wonder. The late Dr C. E. M. Joad used to ask for a synthesis of knowledge, that we might understand better and marvel more at the world in which we live. But, pursuing that same line of thought, we would ask even more insistently for a heightening of the sense of wonder. It is a commonplace that workers in different fields marvel constantly at what they discover.

> *The poet's eye in a fine frenzy rolling*
> *Doth glance from heaven to earth, from earth to heaven;*

but the artist and musician likewise have their ecstasy in the sound and colour of created things, and the man looking down through his microscope will know equally with the man staring up through his telescope the marvels of creation. But indeed the list could be indefinitely extended. Browning gave a reason for fifty hopes and fears:

> *Just when we're safest, there's a sunset-touch,*
> *A fancy from a flower-bell, some one's death,*
> *A chorus-ending from Euripides.*

The patient gardener who at last straightens his back and puts on his coat still carries in his mind the glory of his garden. He passes the eye-specialist who marvels still at the mystery of the human eye. On that same highway is a chemist, a naturalist, a still-surviving craftsman and a lover. If they could meet and discuss together the wonder that is theirs, what a happy meeting that would be. They would know

[2] *Vision and Authority*, p. 352.

something of that strange exaltation when the morning stars sang together and all the sons of God shouted for joy.

The poets continually lament the fact that as we grow we lose our childish wonder. So Wordsworth asked:

> *Whither is fled the visionary gleam?*
> *Where is it now, the glory and the dream?*

Perhaps part of the answer lies in the defective ends of education. We limit its objective too narrowly if we regard it only as the acquisition of knowledge, even though we call it knowledge for living. We define the goal more precisely when we call it response to life. Children must be trained not only to use their brains but their senses. F. S. Pierpoint thanked God:

> *For the joy of ear and eye,*
> *For the heart and mind's delight,*
> *For the mystic harmony*
> *Linking sense to sound and sight.*

The five senses must be encouraged to respond to outside stimuli. Teaching young people to enjoy poetry, to look appreciatively at a painting, to know familiar sights and sounds and scents of the countryside, are steps along that way. To distinguish, in the world of cultural values, the lasting from the transient, the true from the false, the beautiful from the ugly, is to grow sensitive to the colour, sound, and form of this exciting world. No phrase falls more sickeningly on the ear than: 'I couldn't care less.' No words contain a greater indictment of the modern age than 'boredom', 'disillusionment', and 'despair'. A man is really educated in the art of living when he can chuckle and gasp and be astonished as much in old age as in youth.

But an integration of knowledge ought to bring an integration of wonder. The delight a man has in wild flowers and a bird's song must be linked with his wonder at an exquisite work of art, the fleetness of a runner, the courage of the explorer, and the unending surprises of human nature. Only so will he know the folly of describing such a world as the product of blind and purposeless fate. Only then will he understand the awe of Moses when he heard God's voice from a burning bush, or Elijah's exultation when after the mountain storm could be heard a still small voice, or Paul's discovery when the blinding light struck him down upon the Damascus road. He will stand in that transcendent wonder which Thomas Carlyle called worship.

The inducing of such a mood is surely the final end of education. Indeed of the many definitions of man, perhaps the most satisfying is that he is 'a worshipping animal'. Eternity has been set in his heart. 'The spirit of man is the candle of the Lord.' There is no need to fly to the anthropologist to buttress this assertion, but only to show that immemorially man has had objects outside of himself for worship and obedience. Animism, spiritism, tribal deities, world gods, are all stages on his spiritual journey. Even the Buddhist must have his Buddha, though the supreme principle of truth be dissolved in the abstractions of philosophy.

If, as in Soviet Russia, the existence of God be denied, then the State will assume the trappings of the divine and arrogate to itself the worship that belongs to God. Lenin's tomb must do service in place of the empty tomb in the Christian story. St John's last injunction to his little children was to keep themselves from idols; but if God be forsworn, then lesser gods, which are also false gods, must take His place. Paul spoke of those whose god is their belly, and so one might speak of those whose bank account, or position, or sport, is the god of their devotion. Since we become like the gods we worship, it is not inappropriate in modern idiom to speak of the pleasure-loving as the empty-headed, or the over-ambitious as tough, or the money-lovers as hard-faced. The end of education is to lead to the worship of the one true God speaking through His world, through the gifts of men's minds, and fully through His Son. In His worship, as John said in his first epistle, 'we shall be like Him for we shall see him as he is'. This is in consonance with the declaration of A. N. Whitehead that 'moral education is the habitual vision of greatness'. In the worship of God we become good, and goodness is the true flowering of the spirit of man.

Knowledge must pass into wonder and wonder be expressed in worship. This is the essential 'formalism' of education giving it coherence and purpose. Stripped of this 'order', it still gives a man more knowledge and a certain expertise in the handling of it, but it does not lead him to use that knowledge wisely and well. Indeed if vision be lacking, a man may employ his knowledge only in the service of selfish ends. A man's blackguardism can socially be more danger-ous because he is a knowledgeable blackguard. As with men, so with nations. On two occasions in this century a great and educated nation like Germany, with a wrong structure of ideas, could involve itself and others in destructiveness and despair. Lacking vision the people cast off restraint.

Scripture is taught in our schools and there is a daily assembly for worship. When the inwardness of this is recognized, saving both from externality and from death, then religion, true to its derivation, will bind again the differing activities of academic life and thought. Because it supplies meaning, direction, and a final goal, religion supplies order in education from within. John Ruskin once wrote a famous essay on 'The Nature of Gothic', showing that it is the interlacing of many parts into a transcendent unity which compels wonder and induces worship. In that sense of the word, the modern school ought to be Gothic in its academic design.

WORK

The third great sphere in which order must be recovered is in the industrial life of men. Order in home and school must be followed by order in work. In its largest setting this implies a true understanding of social democracy. The danger in the theory of the State as an organism in which the parts serve the whole is that the State becomes an end in itself, demanding allegiance, but offering no goal beyond its own smooth functioning. This is certainly true of Hegel, and in part of the later school of Oxford idealists in England; F. H. Bradley and Bernard Bosanquet held an organic view of the State which hovered perilously on the brink of absorbing the life of the individual within the spirit of the nation. In his *Philosophical Theory of the State*, Bosanquet approaches Hegel's idea of the State as a living mind. But once you talk like this you are on the way to an unwarranted veneration of the State. That way lies the danger both of tyranny and of Caesar-worship. Individualism and Collectivism must learn from each other. The individual must be, in Kant's phrase, 'an end in himself'. He must also in partnership with others work for the common good. That good is not one which the State defines, but which the State serves. It is the good life, and Government can serve it negatively by removing hindrances, and positively by creating the right conditions for its realization. This transcendent good, served by man individually in his private life and corporately as a member of the State, is an antidote to anarchism and to despotism. It allows freedom with responsibility. It adjusts the relation of the part and the whole, the man and the State. But even as it describes the scope of the State it defines its limits. There is a moral order, natural and revealed, which also it must serve.

If men knew and accepted this political philosophy, it would prevent anti-social behaviour in their private lives, and it would also prevent them as workers from seeking private ends without social reference. The worker would know himself to be a member of the whole community. The right to strike would be used responsibly.

Within this larger framework, however, there is today a search for order within industry itself. The story begins perhaps with the publication of Mary Parker Follett's *Dynamic Administration*. It has been assumed far too long that the main incentives in industry are the stick and the carrot. This is the way to treat donkeys but not man. Even so, in great industrial centres calling out for more labour, the advertisements are couched in terms of high wages, short hours, and long holidays. No mention is made of such intangibles as satisfaction in work. Yet industrial psychology in the last quarter of a century has insisted steadily that the best results are obtained when the worker's interest is secured and he knows 'what it is all about'. The experiment conducted at the Hawthorne Works of the Western Electric Company, U.S.A. (1924–32) is now very widely known. The firm began a series of experiments in which the workers' co-operation was secured. Hours were shortened, and other material benefits one by one were introduced. Meanwhile the reactions of the employees as well as the rate of production were steadily noted. Then with the consent of the employees the favourable conditions were removed, and still output was increased. It was found that shorter hours and better conditions were featherweights in the balance against the heavy pull of spiritual factors. If the workers could share in the social experiment, they would remain unaffected by worsened conditions and output would still rise. Give them, however, better conditions but exclude them from co-operation, and with such a shadow on the spirit, production would fall. Similarly, Dr G. Walton in his *Fundamentals of Industrial Psychology*, reporting on a certain inquiry, said that the output of the women rose whether they had rest periods or not during the period of investigation.[3] The reason was that they liked the idea of co-operating in the inquiry. It gave them a sense of importance and this stimulated their activity.

This brings one straight back to a fundamental principle in Mary Follett's industrial philosophy. She maintained that every individual must count as a person and an effective member of his group. It is a dictum which is steadily finding active expression in factories and business houses. The narrow interests of the management and the larger interests of society are both served when workers are treated not as instruments of production but as men.

[3] Pages 123 f.

It has been found that the environment in which people work can raise or depress their spirits. A cheerful distemper on the walls, and the intelligent arrangement of furniture and plant within office, work-shop, and factory, just because they form the whole background of workers' lives, play a large part in shaping their outlook. The value of cleanliness, ventilation, warmth, and good lighting, has been recog-nized in factory legislation, but how great a gulf lies between the minimum legal requirement and the maximum effort of those with vision and capacity! In some industrial undertakings the change from the old order to the new was like the raising of the safety curtain in a pantomime, revealing, in place of a trivial piece of painted cloth, the breath-taking 'transformation scene'. Playing-fields, well-appointed canteens, rest-rooms, first-aid posts, and whatever else promotes material well-being, are recognized at least in larger concerns as the background of the worker's life.

Industrial psychologists have been pressing this same conclusion upon employers for many years. If goods are to be cheap and gener-ally available, mass production will be necessary and many jobs will be monotonous and repetitive. Charlie Chaplin, in his picture 'Modern Times', presented a scathing indictment of large-scale in-dustry which has no body to be kicked and no soul to be damned. The all-seeing eye can watch the hapless slaves of the conveyor belt not only when they are at their work, but also when, pressed by inexorable necessity, they must temporarily leave it. Woe betide the unlucky wight who has not completed his part of the process when the product moves along to the next worker on the belt! Charlie Chaplin ended the film with a fade-out of the figure of the tramp, the factory gates closed behind him, walking down the long road toward the golden sunset.

> *When the artless doctor sees*
> *No one hope, but of his fees,*
> *And his skill runs on the lees,*
> *Sweet Spirit comfort me!*

Robert Herrick might well despair when he had a doctor who could diagnose but could not cure. To escape down a road may be good for one man but not for the children of men. We desire neither to be robots nor tramps. Eric Gill's indictment of factory industrialism was that it deprives a man of freedom, responsibility, ownership, and union. He said it unwearyingly in all his books, and the sting in his attack has not died with his death. He would not give art to the 'arty', because for him it was no mere embellishment to life, but life itself, for it consisted in the right making of things. He believed that the ability and enthusiasm for such work was part of every man's heritage. 'Art', he said, 'is simply the well making of what needs making,' and again: 'Art is collaboration with God in creation.'[4] To be a tramp is to have a certain kind of freedom but no responsibility. When we talk of the goods made available to poor as well as rich by modern industrialism, and proceed to congratulate ourselves on higher standards of living for all, let us at least not be under any delusion about the price we have had to pay. And let us strive mightily, as we are able, to rescue persons from the tyranny of machines. Christopher Dawson said: 'If a man is essentially a tool-using animal, the tool is from the beginning that of the artist no less than that of the labourer.' It is human values we must be intent to salvage. If a person has to do a monotonous piece of work, endlessly repeated, at least let him know his job in relation to all the jobs in the factory. What is more important still, let him know what happens when the goods leave the factory. Where do they go and how do they benefit the community at large? The little girl applying for the least important job in the vast workshop ought not to be shown at once to her place on the bench, but ought to have an opportunity to know her part in the whole concern, and the part of the concern in the whole life of society. Workers, in a word, are persons, and must never be treated as means to an end. There must be no 'bruising of the hapless head of a wronged people yearning to be free'. To stimulate interest and invite co-operation is both wisdom and duty on the part of the management.

There is a second point of equal importance if there is to be order within industry. There must be an identity of interest between management and men within any industrial undertaking. Books like that of J. S. Burnham have shown the importance of the 'managerial revolution'. The new tasks and responsibilities as well as the new status of the manager have been the subject of much inquiry, but not enough has been said about the technique of joint consultation and joint production schemes. When Professor Ghiselli investigated the aims of employees he discovered that wages and hours of labour came only fourth and fifth in importance. Of greater importance still were steady employment, responsibility, freedom, good equipment, and right working conditions. Next to wages and hours came the demand to be treated as persons, to have a voice in management, and to have grievances adjusted.[5]

4 *Art Nonsense and Other Essays.*
5 E. E. Ghiselli, *Personnel and Industrial Psychology*, pp. 438–9.

Schemes of co-partnership and profit-sharing are good, but of themselves are not good enough. There must be actual consultation between management and men.

It is this development which, even more than profit-sharing, is significant for industry as a whole. To improve physical conditions and to stimulate interest is excellent, but the ultimate aim must always be the free interchange of views about the conduct of the firm between management and workers. During the war years, in Great Britain, a notable advance was made. In 1943 there were roughly four thousand five hundred joint production committees in engineering and allied industries. Over ninety per cent of the shipyards had set up yard committees. In the coal-mining industry there were over a thousand pit production committees. The same story could be told in other industries. When there was need, the relevant problems were discussed by regional joint consultative boards whilst trade union district production committees maintained contact with their local committees. This spur of common concentration in satisfying national needs sent up production in a dramatic way.

If the method brought such dividends in war, why should it not succeed in days of peace? There is no need to be scared by bogies. Consultation does not imply the workers' direction of industry. An indefinite number of hands cannot grip the steering wheel. But suspicion persists, and joint production and consultative committees have steadily declined in numbers. Some employers undoubtedly feel that consultation may infringe the prerogatives of management. They wonder whether it will give opportunity to trouble-makers, or prove to be a waste of time. And just as there are workmen who are inveterately suspicious of any move the management may make, and are always disposed to ask, 'What are they up to now?', so there are employers who seem congenitally unable to trust workmen and to value their counsel. Shop stewards are often near-Communist in sympathy and joint consultation committees do not fit into their scheme of things, and trade union officials wonder how it will affect the bargaining prospects.

One thing is certain. Nothing is more essential than increased production, and the more the private profit-making motive is eliminated, the more necessary will be the need to encourage the workers to play their full and proper part in the economic recovery of the nation. This means that there must be joint consultation at local, regional, and national levels. The one goal to which we must steadily move is the identification of interest between management and men in the service of the common good. Industrial team-work in the interests of society

K

is no unworthy slogan for such a time as this. 'Government and co-operation', said Ruskin, 'are in all things the laws of life; anarchy and competition the laws of death.' There was no class struggle, cried someone bitterly, until Marx discovered it. That half-truth does illumine the fact that there is no necessity for struggle within industry, but only for understanding and a common strategy. During the last century the worker was on the defensive, and only through the Trade Union could he pit himself against the power of the employer. In this century he is on the offensive. How will the Giant use his strength? Is it his intention to dominate the situation? There are disquieting symptoms of a willingness to fight 'for my interests, my whole interests, and nothing but my interests'. On occasion there has been not only an impatience with the negotiating machinery and a disposition to force the issue by more drastic methods, but a refusal to face hard economic fact. If a cake is noticeably smaller there is a limit to the size of the pieces that can be cut. On both sides therefore old suspicions and animosities need to be overcome. On both sides there must be the recognition that a changed situation demands a changed technique. On both sides there must be an effort, both of will and of imagination, if industry is to be matched with the hour.

Lastly, the working life of man reveals order when a third postulate is accepted. Workers must be treated as persons and must co-operate with management, but both sides in industry must serve the well-being of society. Price rings, cartels, and all monopolistic practices which maintain private profits at public expense are to be condemned. It is not only necessary for management to play fair with workers, but for trade unions and manufacturers' unions to play fair with society. The ideal in any industry is to co-operate to turn out a worth-while product in which both sides can take an honest pride. This pattern for industry is curiously like the pattern of right relationships in the Kingdom of God. It is an overcoming of sectional jealousies and antagonisms in the recognition that each man counts and that all are needed to serve together in the fulfilment of God's purpose for society. Expressed in such language, it may seem both unreal and impracticable, but this is the agreed conclusion of industrial psychologists. It is a transcript of their contention that the worker must be treated as a person, that management and men must understand each other and work harmoniously, and that the wider interests of society must always be preserved. Slowly men are coming to know that this is morally right, and that what is morally right can also be financially possible and economically expedient.

LEISURE

New technical advances inevitably mean new words in the language. One such word is automation. When factories run almost automatically save for the few who manipulate knobs and levers, there will be a vast increase in leisure time. Some American industrialists talk already of a thirty-hour week. If machines can be invented to replace man-labour, the inference is that man will be free to do other things. Already the process is well begun. In many countries of the West a forty-hour week is normal, and that leaves one hundred and twenty-eight hours at a man's disposal.

It is a mark of our inability to deal with this new situation that we speak of the 'problem' and not the 'opportunity' of leisure. In a recent inquiry conducted by a British newspaper, many contributors said they would welcome increased leisure in order to take on a spare-time job. Even today many eagerly seek overtime because of the extra money it brings to the family exchequer, and doubtless because the extra time would otherwise mean 'time on one's hands'. A more direct proof of this inability to use leisure creatively is shown in the development of the 'mass man'. The Priestleys in their book *Journey down a Rainbow* only emphasize what sociologists describe with apprehension. Mass production in the industrial world is accompanied by mass media of entertainment in the world of leisure. Man is at the 'receiving end' of cinema, radio, television, and popular press. His rôle could be active if he was critical and discriminating in mood; too often, however, he is the passive recipient of pleasure served out to him in bulk. His inner life is so impoverished that fictional characters in radio and television, story, and serial, can be more real to him than live victims of accident, pestilence, persecution, or war. The 'mass man' has his idols on stage, screen, television, radio, and the world of sport. He knows them by their Christian names, swallows with avidity every detail that can be communicated of their personal lives. In fact he is busily watching other lives without actively living his own life. He is a spectator and not an actor in the drama of life.

The process of passivity is hastened by the nature of his working hours. Very often a man's total energies are not needed in the performance of his task; sometimes only the tips of his fingers are required in the repetitive work he endlessly performs until the buzzer brings release. It is entirely fallacious to suppose that if a man's job is monotonous he can find relief in a constructive use of his leisure hours. In practice it is the man who uses his brain during working hours, and more especially in wider fields of interest, who will continue to find creative satisfaction in his leisure time; his mind is sharpened as an instrument for that very purpose. But the man who has work demanding a minimum of mental effort cannot use his leisure constructively because he cannot suddenly become a different person as he walks out of the factory gates. There is a law of atrophy in life. The brain that is allowed to rust becomes rusty. The man who is the slave of a machine in working hours can easily become the slave of a different kind of machine in leisure time. The furniture of a room can be grouped around gramophone, wireless, and television. The book requiring concentration is left unread. Even the weightier daily paper or weekly periodical is left to others. The paper with a maximum of pictures and a minimum of newsprint comes into its own. The back pages with details of sport compete with the strip cartoons for first claim on attention. It is no matter for surprise that glamour (particularly associated with sex), sensational stories (particularly associated with crime), and gossip (particularly associated with popular idols) can often be main ingredients in that reading diet.

If this picture seems overdrawn and if those who protest against it would draw attention, not to indoor facilities for enjoyment, but to the vast increase of opportunities for outdoor-recreation, one can only ask whether this is not a reproduction of the same picture in another setting. The roads choked with cars and motor coaches taking people to popular places of resort, and in a few hours bringing them back again, provoke the same question. Allowing for the fact that man is a gregarious animal, is there sufficient individualization in taste and interest? Are we not in danger of mass suggestion, through mass media, about what we ought to wear, what we ought to eat, and what we ought to enjoy?

In a recent remarkable book, Mr Josef Pieper has expressed his thesis in the title: *Leisure as the Basis of Culture*. Culture lies in the 'intellectual' use of leisure. He draws an interesting distinction between *ratio* and *intellectus* and believes that in the latter is our clue to a perception of life as it is and as it ought to be lived. Perhaps one can press too hard the difference between the mind at work and the mind in repose. Yet there are wider ranges of life that often come through the magic casement of a mind receptive to the wonder and glory of creation. 'Education concerns the whole man, man *capax universi*, capable of grasping the totality of things.' But education depends on the right use of *intellectus* and this in turn on leisure.

It is obvious that idleness is not a synonym for leisure. Idle is derived from an old English word 'idel' signifying empty. The idle man is one who does not know how to use his spare time. When we say he idles it away, we mean that he empties it of all its content. On the other hand, leisure comes from the Latin *licere*, to be allowed, and is defined as the opportunity to do. The implication is of free time eagerly seized because it allows one to do what in working hours could not be done. One noun is passive and one is active. One implies only cessation from work whilst the other suggests a creative mode of living. Idleness is a pause between bouts of activity. Leisure is an activity of the whole sentient being, a response of the spirit to the marvel of life.

Our modern dilemma arises because free time is construed as idleness and not as leisure. The worker is so caught up in temporal processes that even when he stops work it is only as a horse may stop before he starts again. Idleness is the opposite of employment. Each word is necessary to the other. The idle man is 'empty' until again he works and is 'full'. But leisure is not the opposite of any other human state. It is full and satisfying in its own right. The idle man stands on the seen and temporal, but the leisured man on the unseen and the eternal. He has escaped from the time-machine. His soul can grow.

Modern man's inability to use his free time wisely stems from a lack of order. He knows no method whereby his time can be laid out to best advantage. Automation comes to a race that is unprepared for such a gift. We are at the mercy of our own instincts and desires at a time when they can be exploited and abused. We are like the rich farmer who, when he came to a time of retirement, had no constructive ideas. He could only think in the same thought-forms and accept the same categories of value. 'I will pull down my barns', he said, 'and build greater.'

The recent British Royal Commission on Gambling declared that 'the spread of gambling is one of the symptoms of an age in which people have more leisure and cannot or do not know how to make good use of it'. But anti-social practices thrive in man's free time because he lacks a social philosophy of living.

One healthy symptom of our age is that the bewilderment of modern man in his increased free time is known to sociologists and is the subject of active inquiry and comment. The topic is discussed in papers and magazines and treated more formally in treatises and books. As always, diagnosis is simpler than remedy. The disorder is admitted, but how can there be a recovery of order? How can leisure have a pattern?

The immediate answer is that leisure cannot be treated as though it existed apart from work and yielded its own separate solution. If a life has a pattern, then leisure will be included in that wider harmony. Let a man have a sense of obligation to God, to his fellow-men and to his own inner self, and he will follow the guiding principles in his free time as well as in his working hours. A man with an integrated philosophy has an integrated life. He is as disciplined at home as at work. Of him are the lines true:

So shall no part of day or night
From sacredness be free.

Such a philosophy alone can enable a man 'to number his days'. The art of leisure is the art of selection. It depends on the proper use of time. The understanding of time as a concept may keep philosophers endlessly employed; but for the business of living, the important question is not what it is, but what to do with it.

There are three main attitudes to adopt. One is to ignore the question altogether and to treat time with complete carelessness. For the schoolboy, considerations of time are irrelevant; surely 'time will go on for ever'. The tragedy arises when the unthinking attitude of the child persists in after life. There are people who, having become men, do not put away childish things. They ignore the transitoriness of life and the fewness of their days. Then retirement comes as a sudden shock to consciousness. Too late they realize that they have developed no interests apart from work. How many die in their sixties, not because of any fatal disease, but because of an incurable malady of spirit? Their inner life is a great emptiness. They have no special cause for living. Death can claim its own.

There is a second attitude which one must denominate as sheer folly. It is adopted by those who recognize the shortness of time but come to wrong conclusions. The rich farmer declared as an ultimate goal his intention to 'eat, drink and be merry', and God said he was a fool. There is a parallel to that dominical indictment in Paul's words that the Kingdom of God is not eating and drinking, but righteousness and peace and joy in the Holy Spirit. Despite those warnings the rich fool has many followers. There are many undesirable people whose record in the Police Courts is perfectly clean. They are not bad nor vicious; they just squander their time unwisely. Amongst their ranks are people who form wrong social habits such as the heavy gambler and the habitual drunkard. There are people who use sex as an instrument of pleasure and whose barnyard morals seem never to disquiet them. There are people with too low a conception of truth, honour, or the property of others. And in these ranks are to be found all those with vulgar tastes, whose choice of reading, entertainment, and spare time habits, can only impoverish and debase the mind. This is lifting a small corner of a curtain which hides a world in which all the bright lights, the high-pitched voices, the mirthless laughter, the contempt for moral values, do not disguise a cheap and garish approach to life.

Finally there is that right understanding of time which enables a man so to number his days that he gets 'an heart of wisdom'. The three most valuable commodities a man possesses are his time, his money, and his energy. All must be laid out jealously as a miser might reckon his store of gold. This is far removed from a crabbed restriction of life made to fit a moralist's tape-measure. It is an apprehension of life in all its dimensions, and the capacity to enjoy it to the full. It does depend however upon the recognition of order. There is no true freedom without discipline. There is no enjoyment of leisure without an adequate philosophy. To speak of the obligation to God, one's fellow, and oneself, may be to disguise a richly satisfying approach to the concept of time in words too plain and sober. In nontechnical language, it means first of all, in the majestic words of the Westminster catechism, that a man must 'Glorify God and enjoy Him for ever'. The first and last charge upon one's time is the laying out of one's life to the greater glory of God. This involves the keen perception of His presence in the colour, sound, and form of all created things, the recognition of His bounty in the varied gifts of men's minds, the sensitiveness to His word in the lighted page, the saintly life, and the increasing ministry of the Holy Spirit. It is the willingness to respond to such a God in contemplation and activity, in thought and service. This total response breaks down the distinction between sacred and secular, work and leisure, because it is an offering of body, mind, and spirit, which involves the whole life.

Coincident with this apprehension of God is the awareness of others as members of the same family. There is a sense in which only those who are 'adopted' into the mystical body of Christ can be said to be 'no more strangers and foreigners, but . . . of the household of God'. Nevertheless, since each man bears God's image, we are forbidden to look with indifference or hostility into our brother's eyes. Both work and leisure are rightly informed when we bear men's needs in mind and are ready to serve their interests. A second call upon our time therefore is the obligation to give ourselves to some form of community service. The separation of sheep from goats at the Last Judgement is determined not by what we have said but by what we have done. It is the cup of cold water given to the thirsty which reflects the true orthodoxy. John Ruskin in his greatest book seized upon a phrase 'unto this last' from the Parable of the Labourers in the Vineyard. The same amount is paid to the last of those who come to serve, as God pays to the first. There is however another word of our Lord, which offers the human parallel to that Divine initiative; it is the word 'inasmuch', signifying what we must do for the least, even as God does it for the last. 'Inasmuch as ye have done it unto one of the least of these my brethren, ye have done it unto me.' There is service in our work, but service is also demanded in our leisure.

Finally the right understanding of time involves a recognition of our own status as the sons of God. We are not to live three-dimensionally in a four-dimensional universe. 'What is man, that thou art mindful of Him?' The answer is not a being of no consequence, but one who has been set only a little lower than the angels. It follows that 'worldliness' is to be condemned because it strait-jackets a man, confining him in too-narrow limits, and leaving a citizen of two worlds the occupant of only one. The word recreation must be split up if the original sense is to be rediscovered. Re-creation involves that proper use of the body and its powers which renews a man physically; it implies that proper use of all his faculties which renews him mentally; it means that whole response to spiritual stimuli which makes him a new creature. A right use of leisure therefore lies at the heart of all good living. For having a good time means having time to be good. It is a discovery of our true nature and therefore of our high calling.

When Matthew Arnold complained that we had no shelter to grow ripe, no leisure to grow wise, he pointed out our consequent loss:

> *Too fast we live, too much are tried,*
> *Too harass'd to attain*
> *Wordsworth's sweet calm, or Goethe's wide*
> *And luminous view to gain.*

The return to that lost estate lies in the return to a Christian pattern of living. Isaac Watts (as emended by Wesley) asked surprisingly:

> *And shall we then for ever live*
> *At this poor dying rate?*

He had good reason for surprise, since there was One who came expressly that we might have life and that we might have it more abundantly.

Section IV

THE DEBATE ON GOD

CHAPTER XI

THE STORY OF TWO GARDENS

THE argument of these pages leaves one overshadowing question: Has the Church a saving word for man's condition? Mankind is impatient for the answer. The long debate on man which has waxed furiously since Renaissance days has brought us, through the furnace of events as much as through the ferment of thought, to realize the inadequacy of all forms of humanism. Man is not able unaided to deliver himself. There is an internal contradiction in his nature which is not to be resolved in the class-room or in the laboratory or in the Council Chamber. He all-unwittingly waits on God. The cure for his sickness is spiritual. It lies in a theology of grace. However much the cultivated may resist the hard saying, it is God who must intervene decisively on behalf of man. Only as man avails himself of the Divine initiative, is guided by Divine revelation, and is empowered by the Divine Spirit, can he walk and not stumble.

At this hour of man's profound understanding of his need, the results of a hundred years of intensive criticism have left the Bible unimpaired in its authority. As David H. C. Read in his book on *The Christian Faith* has truly said: 'As a result of the most intense labour of research we may have the greatest confidence in the authority and integrity of the records. No miraculous claim is made by most Christians for the reporting of these events, but it has stood up amazingly to the most rigorous critical examination.'[1] Our fathers were tempted to tremble at the sound of 'Higher Criticism', but sound research only destroys the false and establishes the true. More than ever the Bible stands as the word of God, and 'whosoever will, let him take the water of life freely'.

Some years ago an attractively produced book was published under the title *The Bible Designed to be Read as Literature.* It is a pleasant book for a casual hour, so long as it is always understood that the Bible was never designed to be read as literature. It is from first to last the record of the dealings of God with man as they have taken place through the history of a single people. Since it is the record of a people's emergence from tribal beginnings, it is in one aspect the record of their slowly-developing ideas of God. There was a time when God to the Israelites was little more than a war God, jealous of His own honour, careful to secure His people, and therefore im-

---

[1] Page 28.

placable towards their foes. The slaying of the Amalekites, the stoning of Achan and his whole family, the tearing in pieces of Agag, are part of an early conception of God in which truth was mingled with error. Gradually, with the passage of centuries, the understanding of God was purified and enlarged until, with the great prophets of the eighth century B.C., the moral attributes of God became known. His wisdom, righteousness, and holiness, made Him the one true God of all the earth. Revelation is the drawing back of a veil, and in Jesus Christ the veil was wholly thrown back and the full nature of God disclosed.

That is the story from the manward angle. Within those historical dimensions, however, the whole divine drama is enacted. The Bible might well be called 'the story of the two gardens'. It begins with a garden in which man and woman aspired to be as God, desiring the knowledge of good and evil, setting their own desires above obedience to God. Sin is always the assertion of self, and not of God, as the centre of life and interest. It is the creature becoming the creator. It is the dependent seeking independence. Inevitably it means Paradise lost.

Adam is but the Hebrew term for man, and it is mankind which by its tragic rejection of God's way has brought sorrow and suffering upon itself. The solidarity of mankind means that disobedience to God involves not only the evildoer but the community of which he is part. Its consequences can extend down the generations. The truth of Genesis must not be sought by laboratory or clinical tests; it is established day by day in every newspaper of the world.

But what can be done for man in his lost estate? The Old Testament propounds three main answers. First the Prophet says to his people that repentance from sin and righteousness of life provide the twofold escape from his misery. But the people reply despairingly that whilst for prophet-souls such a solution may be practicable, for the ordinary man the air is too rarefied, the summit too steep for attainment. The Priest then comes with the comforting assurance that if contrition is expressed in Temple sacrifice, all will be well. But the answer is too easy to satisfy the tormented. Micah speaks for the inarticulate many when he thunders: 'Wherewith shall I come before the Lord and bow myself before the high God? Shall I come before Him with burnt offerings, with calves of a year old? Will the Lord be pleased with thousands of rams, or with ten thousands of rivers of oil?' Micah knew what the Lord required of him and sacrifices were not included.

Finally came the lawgiver to assert that in keeping the Law a man could satisfy God and his own conscience. At first the answer seemed right and inevitable. Psalm 119 is one long paean of praise for 'testimonies' which are 'wonderful' and righteous judgements which endure for ever. But alas! the discovery of Paul was anticipated by long generations who had found the Law to become a bondage and its standard to mock their vain endeavours. They had found that the good they would they did not, and the evil they would not, that they did.

The Old Testament despite its noble attempts to deliver man, leaves him in his old predicament. No four lines more aptly sum up his hopeless state than the profound truth of a nursery rhyme:

> *Humpty Dumpty sat on a wall,*
> *Humpty Dumpty had a great fall,*
> *All the King's horses and all the King's men*
> *Could not put Humpty together again.*

Everything is there, including the Fall. Prophet, Priest, and Lawgiver, all the King's horses and all the King's men, try in vain to restore his lost estate. But the angel with the flaming sword keeps his guard too well. Man cannot guide his fellow man back into the garden. Isaac Watts did not overdraw his picture when he spoke of wretched sinners plunged in a gulf of dark despair,

> *Without one cheerful beam of hope,*
> *Or spark of glimmering day.*

Humanly speaking, all that could be done was done, and it was not enough. The barrier between man and God had proved impassable. Now any move must lie with God Himself.

The New Testament is the answer to the dilemma of man posited by the Old Testament. What we could not do for ourselves, God did for us. Still to quote Watts:

> *With pitying eyes the Prince of Peace*
> *Beheld our helpless grief:*
> *He saw, and—O amazing love!*
> *He flew to our relief.*

The dispute between Arius and Athanasius was over the most important topic in the world. In the end everything depends on the view you take of Christ's person. You may load Him with honours and concede Him every earthly title, but unless He comes as the 'fulness of the Godhead bodily', your adulation means nothing. If He is only a man, even the greatest of humankind, He can only do what man can do. His teaching about God, man, sin, and eternal life may or may not be true; there is no certainty because there is no absolute authority. Certainly His claims fall to the ground. With His contemporaries we are justified in asking, how can this man claim to forgive sins? He is neither able to give rest to the heavy-laden nor protection to the flock. As Athanasius realized, so much depends on a diphthong.

If He was man, then His death was only martyrdom, and His resurrection the daring intuition of a small company. No theology, either incarnationist or redemptionist, could be built on such foundations. Though a man in his strength towers up to heaven, he is infinitely weaker than One who came down from heaven and was 'contracted to a span'. The one creedal basis for the constituent communions of the World Council of Churches is the acceptance of Christ as God and Saviour. Anything less would undermine the unchanging witness of the Church to her Lord as the express image of God. When God speaks fully it is in the Word made flesh. In the life of Jesus we see in time what God is like in all eternity.

Those who sneer at so-called changes in the climate of Christian opinion might well marvel at the fact that, whereas our much vaunted scientific thought changes its emphasis so rapidly, the ancient Creeds still express for Christians the substance of their belief. Gustaf Aulén in his *Christus Victor* has been able justly to speak of the typical Christian view which he calls the 'classic' idea of Atonement. On this basis the first inquiry is to ask what God has done. The New Testament becomes the revelation of the mighty act of God in Christ Jesus. That is why Christ is *Christus Victor*—the One who by His death and rising again triumphs over sin, death, and the devil. Aulén quotes the mighty words of Martin Luther concerning Jesus as Lord: 'What is it now to be a Lord? It is this: that He has redeemed me from sin, from the devil, and from death and all woe. For before, I had not yet had any Lord, nor King, but had been held captive under the devil's power, doomed to death, ensnared in sin and blindness. . . . Now therefore these tyrants and gaolers are all crushed, and in their place is come Jesus Christ, a Lord of Life, righteousness, all good and holiness, and He has snatched us poor lost men from the jaws of hell, won us, made us free, and brought us back to the Father's goodness and grace.'

This view can best be set forth in dramatic terms. God came down from heaven as babe, carpenter, and preacher. In His own Person He met the combined onslaught of all the powers of evil. At the moment of their seeming triumph they were totally defeated. His victory was so entire that Luther could describe it as a victory over sin, death, the curse, wrath, Law, and the Devil.

Behind the obscure reference to the descent into hell which found its way into the Apostles Creed lies a pictorial representation of that triumph. The medieval writers had their own interpretation. Christ's victory, they asserted, was so complete that He was able to harrow hell and to do there what He pleased.

This activity of divine love can succeed where prophet, priest, and lawgiver failed. Because it is greater than sin, it brings the assurance of forgiveness, deliverance, and renewal. Because it is greater than death, it brings the promise of eternal life; the power which raised up Jesus from the dead shall raise us up also with Him. Because it is greater than the devil, it offers proof of final victory. Thomas Carlyle's translation of Luther's mighty hymn sets the proper mood—

> And let the prince of ill
> Look grim as e'er he will,
> He harms us not a whit:
> For why? His doom is writ;
> A word shall quickly slay him.

The barrier man had raised, and which he was powerless to surmount, has been removed by God's own action. Henceforward man in his guilt and helplessness can know forgiveness and restoration. God was in Christ reconciling the world to Himself. There are no repairs and renewals. The old Adam is gone; there is a new man in Christ Jesus.

History therefore becomes eschatological. It is loaded with new meaning. In a true sense the Last Things are present. The Last Judgement is here and now. Theological writers are fond of speaking of a victory won which leaves us with only 'mopping up' operations to do. The Devil is on a tether and is in fact at the end of his tether. The doom of evil has been pronounced, and now history waits upon the Parousia. God is already enthroned and at His own day and hour will make it evident.

Is this sort of theological language consonant with the facts? The Christian Church is still a minority of the world's population, and the increase in population outstrips the increase in Church membership. Communism is steadily on the march and hundreds of millions accept its defiant atheism. More ominous still is the lack of spiritual vitality in Christian countries. On the European continent, and in Great Britain especially, the practising Christians are in a minority. Even that is not the end of the matter. I remember once hearing the late Dean Inge say of the Christian Church in Great Britain that he could bear the thought of a mere ten per cent of the population taking the Faith seriously. After all was not God willing to save Sodom and Gomorrah if ten righteous men could be found? What distressed him was to think that in that small minority so many were timid and unadventurous, and so few were disciplined in mind and heart and will. In his judgement they did not commend the Faith that they professed. Who can deny the force of that indictment?

The Bible, however, still speaks of the divine sacrifice made once for all, whereby we have been 'delivered from the dominion of darkness and transferred to the Kingdom of His beloved Son' (R.S.V.). We are in a new age, and despite all seeming evidence to the contrary, the battering of hostile forces is but the thunder of waves beating upon the base of an impregnable rock.

On national occasions certain buildings are floodlit. Under that strong searchlight hidden beauties are revealed and the whole outline of the structure is fully seen. So it is that the finished work of Christ enables us to know both the nature of God and the nature of the world in which we live. In that divine light we can see the moral structure of the universe. We can know that goodness is stronger than evil, beauty than ugliness, and truth than lies. It is a moral order in which we cannot ultimately fight against the truth but only for it. In the stern words of Jesus: 'Whosoever shall fall on this stone shall be broken: but whosoever it shall fall on it will grind him to powder.'

Moreover it is a world in which a remedy for sin has been found, so that a man need no longer be burdened by a sense of guilt and moral impotence. In God's world, by God's grace, he can live as God's child. The stars that fight against Sisera are leagued upon his side. The goads that resist the kicking of the wilful are become a spur to moral action. He is 'more than conqueror'.

The New Testament not only asserts this, but illustrates it in the closing book of the Bible. The Apocalypse was written at a time when Domitian outvied Nero in his savage persecution of the Christians. During those last four years of his reign, Christian blood was so foully shed that the hearts of many failed them at the things that were coming to pass on the earth. It was in that evil hour that the writer of the Revelation declared the Roman Empire to be the Beast. Behind the Beast, he said, was the Devil stirring it to ever greater enormities. But the Beast would be destroyed and the Devil cast into a bottomless abyss. In the end there would be a horseman, a solitary horseman, and on his garment and his thigh, a name written: 'King of Kings and Lord of Lords.' None can wholly disentangle an imagery so rich yet so obscure. Nevertheless the substance stands out plainly. The essential meaning is not to be denied. The Roman Empire is the Beast and the Beast will perish; the Devil will be cast into a bottomless abyss; there will remain One who is King of Kings and Lord of Lords.

The book ends in a city which is a garden. There is a river whose waters are clear as crystal and on each bank there are trees whose leaves are for the healing of the nations. The river itself proceeds from the throne of God and on the throne is the Lamb. Ten thousand times ten thousand take up the new song: 'Worthy is the Lamb that hath been slain to receive power and riches, and wisdom, and might, and honour, and glory and blessing.' The Bible ends fittingly in prose, poetry, and music. All are needed to portray the Lamb, slain and alive for evermore, who receives the worship of His saints. The closing note is a note of music. It is the ecstatic song of the redeemed.

Here then is God's story of two Gardens! It begins with man's disobedience and the dread consequences. It speaks of man's inability to save himself. It tells of a mighty deliverance wrought by God Himself. It ends with a second Garden in which God consummates all things, that He may be all in all. In that final revelation of His power, history is not finished but fulfilled.

There are two possible rôles to adopt in any drama. One can watch it or take part in it. One can be either a spectator or a player. It is possible objectively to watch the great drama of God unfolding itself. Eden is a lovely myth albeit true. The wilderness, the kingdom, the exile, the return are main ingredients in the story of a Semite people in which prophet, priest, and law-giver play their individual parts. Bethlehem, Nazareth, Galilee, Jerusalem, and Calvary have haunting significance in the memory; they create again the image of the young Prince of Glory, who, splendid, passed our way. History, because of His coming, has been split in two. The spectator watches the new words in the world's dictionary because the years are *anni domini*. He notes the changing climate of thought and mode of behaviour. He sees the altered status of woman and child, and even, confusedly, is aware of the disturbing impact of the saints in all the ages, the saints who judge the world. Out of the movement of thoughts and events he may acknowledge the moral order and the reality of absolute values. Even more, he may see in a detached way the hand of God in history

L

and give intellectual assent to His Person and Lordship. Following the logic of his thought, he may believe that God 'speaks at length the final word', and 'ushers in the triumph hour'. Even so, seeing all, he sees nothing. He does not even remain a spectator for ever, since all are involved, and at the end 'we must all be made manifest before the judgement-seat of Christ; that each one may receive the things done in the body, according to what he hath done, whether it be good or bad'.

It is the wisdom of believers to recognize that the story of Adam is our story. We also have eaten his particular fruit. We have been guilty of disobedience and known its consequences. We believe in original sin, just as we believe in original virtue, because we know of an internal contradiction in our very natures. There is 'the upward reach' and there is also the downward gravitational pull. The humanists may romanticize about our capacity to arrive at Erewhon, but we know what the word is in reverse. It seems a far more sober estimate to speak of our 'fallen' nature, and so to know both our limits and our possibilities.

We do not quarrel with the attempt of prophets, priests, and lawgivers to deliver their fellow-men, but we are under no delusion about their helplessness. They have come to us with precisely the same age-long result. Sometimes the name has been different. Scientists, educationists, politicians, have come to deliver us, but our bondage has remained. Humpty Dumpty has become terrifyingly real. He spells his name as we do our own.

But we have also known that what we cannot do for ourselves, nor others do for us, God has accomplished on our behalf. Because of His mighty action, we have known forgiveness of sins and deliverance from the thraldom of evil habit. We sing with Charles Wesley

> *He breaks the power of cancelled sin,*
> *He sets the prisoner free.*

A love that is stronger than sin and death is strong both to cleanse and to renew.

We take eagerly all the new titles in the New Testament. Because we are new creatures, we have a new song in our mouths, and all things have become new. We tread a new and living way, and walk in the expectation of that new heaven and earth which are to come. We believe not in *finis* but in τέλος. God whose victory is secure holds history within his grasp. In His time and in His own way His sovereignty will be known to us. 'Glory' will end 'what grace began'.

It is the Church's task to make men know they are participants in the drama, that they may also know the riches of their inheritance.

The Word of God therefore is addressed to the need of men. It speaks of man's plight and the salvation which is through faith, of the victory that is ours, and the glory which shall be revealed.

But there is the Word within the Word. Martin Luther spoke of the Bible as Christ's cradle. In it is the Word made flesh. From many quarters today we are confronted with the need for meeting God face to face. As Martin Buber has said, 'all real life is meeting'; it is I and Thou. This is the theme of the personalists, of the Christian existentialists, and of the neo-Calvinists. They speak, in Brunner's words, of a 'divine-human encounter'. The existential moment is the moment of response to the living God, and if life is lived existentially, that response is continual. Such time is not to be measured by the tick of a clock, but by the grappling of God and man in that wrestling from which a blessing always comes. Here all the great souls are at one. It is said by Paul, Augustine, and Luther, and freshly emphasized by Pascal, Dostoevsky, and Kierkegaard. But indeed it is the heritage of the whole Christian Church, for the Jerusalem which is above is free and is the mother of us all. It is a Gospel which contains the evangelicalism of catholicity and the catholicity of protestantism. It is both catholic and evangelical, and it is greater than both. It is the living Word demanding a living response.

CHAPTER XII

THE MANY AND THE ONE

ONE sign of a revived interest in religion is that men are finding it intolerable to think of a mindless universe in which there is neither purpose nor order. But it is equally unsatisfying to predicate order, intelligence, and design, and still to assert that there is no God. The recovery of a sense of order in the world, and the active search for it in the family, education, work, and leisure, are indications of a revival of interest in religion. Perhaps even more significant than successful evangelistic campaigns is the reaction from the sterility of agnosticism, and the increasing readiness to accept a theistic explanation for the order underlying creation.

But a question still remains. Assuming the hypothesis of an active God, how does He work? More particularly, how can the order discernible in the earth, and in the life upon it, be related to His all-embracing purpose? Has the Christian Faith a relevant word to say as it confronts contemporary thought?

There is a word, a unifying word, and it lies in our Lord's teaching on the Kingdom of God. At the Amsterdam Council of the Christian Churches a sharp division of opinion about the Kingdom was created by theologians, chiefly Continental, who regarded it as lying beyond a space-time order and therefore not to be enjoyed in this world; it is at God's disposal, they said, and man can only wait. In his remarkable book *Man in this World*, Hans Zehrer speaks for this school. Acutely he diagnoses our modern ills. Trenchantly he speaks of modern demonic forces, the end of science and the crisis of perception. But he has no confidence in a this-world virility of the Church. 'Churches must again pass as other-worldly and alien.' 'The individual Christian best renders service to his age by his asceticism and his separateness.'[1] This German theological emphasis met strong resistance from American theologians who insisted that this world is the place for man's toil and not his retreat. Barth and Niebuhr exchanged published letters, and though each wrote moderately the Atlantic rolled between. To many it seemed again the issue between quietism and activism, a waiting upon God and a working for Him.

Nevertheless, the issues are not so clear cut. Continental and American theologians alike would say with Luther, '*sola fide, sola gratia*'. Both accept the fact that the Kingdom is at God's disposal.

[1] op. cit., page 312.

The only vital difference is whether the Kingdom is realizable at all in time. We live in that part of the 'story of two gardens' in which our salvation has been secured and our victory won. Must we therefore wait as a separated people until God speaks once more and finally, or is there still a task to be accomplished?

Professor C. H. Dodd, in a number of books, has set this matter on a biblical basis. Jesus came preaching the Gospel of the Kingdom of God, and the first public announcement was to His own people in the Nazareth synagogue. In startled silence they heard Him say the prophecy of Isaiah was at last fulfilled in His own mighty works—and by signs and wonders, they would know that the Kingdom had come. The Kingdom could not be attained by hard endeavour. There must be, as in the case of the Rich Young Ruler, the casting away of any bauble that prevented one from grasping the greater prize. A repentance that signified a turning from self to God and to a child-like faith in God's grace was the essential of entrance. Except, in your willingness to commit yourselves trustingly to God, you become as little children, you shall not enter. There is nothing weak or passive about this surrender. The Kingdom of God suffers violence, and the violent take it by storm. Nevertheless the violence is not the laying siege to a city, for the city's gates are already open. It is rather the complete emptying of oneself that one may be filled with all the fullness of God. For the Kingdom does not come to the stout in heart but only to the poor in spirit. It is the Father's good pleasure to give us the Kingdom. Jesus could say to His critics, that if, by the finger of God, He cast out devils, then had the Kingdom come upon them. And on another occasion He said to the unfriendly that the Kingdom of God was in their very midst—a statement which has equal truth when translated 'the Kingdom of God is within you'. This Kingdom is like a treasure hid in a field, for which all else must be sold. It is a pearl of great price, beside which other pearls are as nothing. It is a treasury, from which a man may bring out things new and old. All this Charles Wesley understood when he wrote:

> *Jesus, if still the same Thou art,*
> *If all Thy promises are sure,*
> *Set up Thy kingdom in my heart,*
> *And make me rich, for I am poor;*
> *To me be all Thy treasures given,*
> *The Kingdom of an inward heaven.*

The Kingdom, therefore, in a true sense has already come. We do not have to lift God upon His throne; He does not have to wait for the concerted effort of a united Church. 'The Lord God omnipotent reigneth'; in the majestic words of Jeremiah, 'A glorious throne set on high from the beginning is our sanctuary' (R.S.V.). The kingdom of God is His kingly rule, and the laws of the Kingdom are already in operation. The scientist, the psychologist, the historian, trace part of the pattern. Men, finding order in their particular fields of study, steadily discover the nature of the universe; they throw their search-lights on the laws of the Kingdom. But the shape of those laws is supremely revealed in the teaching of Jesus, interpreted by His life, death, and resurrection. The philosophic triad of absolute values is truth, beauty, and goodness, and the Pauline theological variant is faith, hope, and love. But as the apostle wisely recognized, the greatest of these is love. This is the very substance of the laws. By this we know we have passed from death to life, because we love; and conversely, by this we know we have passed from life to death, because we hate.

The King is on His throne; the laws of the Kingdom are already in operation; and, thirdly, the victory is already secured. The 'one obla-tion of Himself once offered' is a 'full, perfect, and sufficient sacrifice for the sins of the whole world'. We cannot forgive ourselves, justify ourselves, or deliver ourselves. There is, however, a 'victory which overcometh the world, even our faith'. This faith is in Him who was dead and is alive for evermore, the Lord of life and the Conqueror of death.

Finally, the possessions of the Kingdom are already available. John Addington Symonds, writing under the sunny skies of Italy in 1893, spoke of a time to come when there would be men 'With flame of free-dom in souls And light of knowledge in their eyes'. But we can have that freedom and that knowledge now. There is no need to wait for his confident forecast of a time when every life shall be a song and all the earth be paradise. A million years hence people will not know more of the peace that passeth understanding, the power that makes us stronger than the strong, or the joy that nothing can disturb. All things are ours, and we are Christ's, and Christ is God's.

The Kingdom, then, is already in our midst, and geographically it covers the earth. God's writ runs through His universe; His laws are binding everywhere. All may partake His triumph and enjoy their inheritance. But the Kingdom of God is the realm of God, and that is not to be defined in acres but in men. The present Kingdom is also a coming Kingdom. Jesus spoke of it as a mustard seed, which, being less than all seeds, yet becomes a tree in which the birds may rest. It is leaven, which, hidden in three measures of meal, leavens the whole. We are bidden to pray 'Thy Kingdom come, Thy will be done, in earth as it is in Heaven'. The Kingdom comes as more and more people come into the Kingdom. Its growth is not to be measured from pole to pole but from heart to heart. The Kingdom stands and grows as more and more of His creatures own His sway. No country can be called Christian, but in every country where men and women love God and do His will, the Kingdom has its citizens.

This carries its own implication. The Kingdom does not come by wise legislation, sound education, enlightened politics. It comes when men acknowledge God as King, obey His laws, share His victory, and possess His riches. The Christian therefore has no blue-print of an earthly paradise. He does not start from that point. He believes that when men are in a right relationship with God there follows the better society for which men long. He does not, therefore, dream of the world as it might be, but of people as they might be. The Christian believes that once they seek the Kingdom of God and His righteousness, these other things will be added unto them. Get the priorities right, and the health, peace, and well-being which men seek will follow as a consequence.

It follows that in the Christian theory of politics the State can never by itself bring men into the Kingdom. That gift is not at its disposal. It can hinder the encroachment of evil in public life. It can limit the baleful effects of anti-social habits and practices by law. It can also secure the right conditions for the good life. It can do this directly through wise legislation, and indirectly through the voluntary and statutory bodies within it. Right order within the family, education, industry, and leisure, can quicken the perception of absolute values, and predispose a man to think in terms of ultimate ends rather than immediate satisfaction.

This becomes more obvious when one thinks in concrete terms. If the John Smiths of the world were born into families in which the members gave and received as mutual beneficiaries within the bonds of respect, affection, and trust, if their education prepared them to receive truth from any quarter and to know all truth to be a unity in its disclosure of God and His purposes, if they engaged in work where proper concern for private interests and private profits was not held to be incompatible with a public-spirited concern for the common good, and if they were taught constructively to use spare time and not to 'kill it', might one not legitimately suppose them to be well prepared to understand the dimensions of the good life?

Already, in a theological phrase, they know the uncovenanted mercies of God. They are beyond the jungle of unregulated appetites; they are within the fair pastures of the King's country, where acknowledgement of order gives style to living. When Oliver Cromwell defeated Lesley at Dunbar, he wrote in a letter to William Lenthall: 'The dimensions of this mercy are above my thoughts. It is, for ought I know, a crowning mercy.' Even so, those who know the rhythm of living have still to know the essence of life; it is the crowning mercy, and it lies within the Christian covenant. When John Smith stands perceptive in God's orderly world, there still remains the confrontation with God. For that dread meeting, he needs but to acknowledge God's self-giving by presenting himself as a living sacrifice which alone can be acceptable to the divine Lord. In this committal of himself to God, in mind, heart, and will, he receives the gift of 'eternal life'. The good life has become his own, because he has stretched out an empty hand for what God alone is able to give.

This is the covenant of grace whereby, because a man acknowledges the divine Lordship, he comes into a new and living relationship with God and with his fellow-men. Old things have passed away. He has become a new creation. He bends the knee to a King who is also Father. He consciously obeys the laws of the Kingdom. He appropriates to himself the fruits of that victory achieved once and for all. He enjoys the privileges of one who by his own action has placed himself within the kingly rule of God.

The proclamation of this good life has been entrusted to the Church alone. 'We are ambassadors for Christ, God making His appeal through us. We beseech you on behalf of Christ, be reconciled to God' (R.S.V.). Because the Church has this unique commission, it has been divinely fashioned for its task. In God's eyes, the Church is not many but one.

The Church is the body of Christ; it is His bride, and His one habitation. There are diversities of gifts and functions. The Church, since it is not dependent upon a Book, a Creed, a Ritual, a Building, or a separated Ministry, for its existence, can be described in the New Testament as meeting in a house, or a city, or a province. Although Church labels describe to us the particular forms of Christian worship and dogma, they do not mean that Christians who bear other labels than our own are outside the Church, but only that they are in other divisions of the same great army. To limit one's attention to one particular part of the Church is to fail to see the one Church which has many parts.

The Church perpetuates the incarnate work of our Blessed Lord, bringing God to men, and bringing men to God. And since it is of God, it has His endowment. There is one Lord, one Faith, one Baptism. There is the one Word—preached from the pulpit, dramatized in the Sacraments, symbolized in art and music and ritual, set forth in creed and dogma, expressed in life and service, but always the one Word of the one God. There is the one Holy Spirit guiding the Church into all truth. There is the one way to tread, which, in the words of John, is the true and living way. There is the one adversary to face, and there is the one victory over sin and death. And because the Church is one, immortal, universal, indestructible, there is for all believers the one ringing assurance, that against this militant fellowship of those who love and serve Christ as Lord, the very powers of hell shall not prevail.

We are familiar nowadays with the slogan that we must not think nationally but internationally. By that we do not mean that people must cease to have regard for or pride in their own communities, but that their interest must not stop at the boundaries of their own countries. Narrow, exclusive nationalism in politics and economics has proved a dangerous and mischievous doctrine, because it is too limited in view. Men are called upon to be citizens not only of their own country, but of the world. In the same way, the time is past when Christians can think comfortably only in terms of their own particular part of the Church. They are challenged to think not denominationally, but ecumenically. Their loyalty to a particular Church must not, and need not, disturb their allegiance to the world-wide Church. In the glorious words of Paul, we must know that we are no more 'strangers and foreigners, but fellow-citizens with the saints, and of the household of God; and are built upon the foundation of the apostles and prophets, Jesus Christ himself being the chief corner stone'.

This is indeed a rich and inspiring conception of the Church. Though men for various reasons come into one section of the Church, they pass through that particular door into the Church universal. They become one with all the followers of Christ in every age. They are in the same company and share the same traditions as Paul, Augustine, Luther, Knox, and Wesley, as well as the unnumbered multitude of unknown saints who in their day and generation walked humbly with their God. For they belong not only to the Church visible and militant, but to the Church invisible and triumphant—both to the great company of those who love and serve God on earth and to that greater company who love and serve Him in Heaven. I remember saying once to a faithful parish priest: 'Don't you ever feel depressed when so very few come to your early communion service?' 'Few?' he said, 'few?—There is all the company of Heaven singing "Holy, Holy, Holy, is the Lord of Hosts"!'

Does this unity involve the idea of uniformity? Must there be not only one flock but one fold? Quite certainly the Holy Spirit is leading the Church into a unity of spirit. The Ecumenical Movement, through Conference, Council, and Communion, has made us aware not only of our 'unhappy divisions', but of what each Church has to contribute to the common stock. At first, Churches found to their surprise how much they had in common. Then at Evanston, the 1954 World Assembly of Churches found how deep-rooted differences still persist. It was a proof that members of the same family were coming to have more than a superficial knowledge of each other. Such understanding only deepened the realization that Churches need each other in common quest and discovery. It is grievous to think that, in Christendom, Churches seem to present a divided front to the outsider. 'Which of you are we to believe?' says the heckler in the open-air meeting. He follows this up by asking how a divided Church can work for a united world. Christians are even more fully aware of their weakness. To have many separate Christian Communions means to waste men, buildings, and resources. We cannot deploy our forces to meet the challenge of a defiant secularism. We cannot adapt ourselves to a highly mobile age. Christian work in non-Christian countries suffers intolerably because we come to it denominationally. What special significance can 'Methodist', 'Baptist', 'Congregationalist', 'Presbyterian', or 'Anglican' have to an African bushman, a Hindu outcast, or a Chinese coolie? Tradition, liturgy, hymnology, signify little to those whose own ethos is so sharply different. In non-Christian countries the native Christians will discover in time their own mode of Churchmanship and it will not be riven by alien ecclesiastical traditions.

Doth this mean that union must be a short-term objective for all the Churches? A strait-jacketed, uniform organization is by no means a self-evident blessing. Too much can be sacrificed for its attainment. The gulf between Catholicism (whether Anglo, Roman, or Eastern) and Protestantism is too wide for an easy jump. The Report of the Anglican Commission on Christian Doctrine (1937) talks in authentic Catholic tones when it declares that 'the acceptance of an Order of Ministry cannot be based on considerations of evangelistic effectiveness alone apart from any regard for continuity and unity. The life of the Church is continuous from generation to generation: continuity of ministerial commission embodies in the sphere of order the principle of Apostolicity in the sense of continuous mission from Christ and the Father. The ministers of the Church in all later generations have possessed a pastoral authority as themselves holding commission from the Lord in succession to the Apostles, and the status of minister in this succession has been guaranteed from one generation to another by a continuously transmitted commission; consequently to preserve continuity in this respect is at all times of great importance'.

This is strange language to a Protestant. He is forced to deny all its main assumptions. He does not believe in a mechanical theory of apostolic succession. He may accept episcopacy as of the *bene esse* but not as of the *esse* of the Church. It can never be to him an *essential* form of Church government, and even when he accepts it, he does not agree that constitutional episcopacy (as in the American Methodist Church) is *ipso facto* inferior to monarchical episcopacy. He cannot therefore accept the Catholic teaching that episcopal ordination alone can give validity to ministerial orders. Nor can he for a moment agree that only the episcopally ordained are valid celebrants of the Sacraments. He winces at the very idea that only those who are confirmed can properly receive the sacred elements. One step follows logically from the other, but he would deny the whole original premise. He has not so learned Christ.

The New Testament speaks of the Church organically. It is one body, though it has many members. Jesus Christ is the head, and as Dr T. W. Manson argued in his book *The Church's Ministry*, that means that His ministry alone is essential and constitutive; 'All others are dependent, derivative and functional.' There is no room therefore for exclusiveness. None can claim a valid ministry which makes others invalid. The Protestant does not deny the validity of priestly orders, but he extends that priesthood to all believers. The minister differs from the layman only in the nature of his call and the exercise of his functions. By an inward constraint of the Holy Spirit he feels called to separate himself wholly to the work of the Ministry. He cries out, 'Woe is me if I preach not the Gospel,' and his own call is confirmed and recognized by the Church, and by the signs which follow his ministry. Holding these views he cannot accept re-ordination as the price of re-union, for that would betray his deepest convictions about the nature of the Ministry and the validity of his call.

None will deny the importance of continuity in the Christian tradition. The stating of hierarchical authority in Catholic terms doubtless strengthened the Church in its struggle against heresies within and foes without. Under that system countless millions of Christians have been nourished by God and used by Him in the service of His Kingdom. It bears witness, in the words of the Anglican Commission (1937), to 'an essential identity of doctrine, a continuity of order, and a fellowship in missionary duty'.

Nevertheless to its emphasis on continuity needs to be added the Protestant stress on the Crown Rights of the Redeemer, the discipline and judgement of the Word, salvation by faith alone, the apostolic succession of the faithful and the priesthood of all believers. Neither Catholic nor Protestant possesses the whole truth, but each has undeniable marks of the Holy Spirit's guidance. Each needs must learn from the other.

All of us admire the scientific spirit in its passion for truth and its integrity of purpose. But the 'scientific attitude' is repellent, because even in its vaunted rationality it is hard, dogmatic, and self-righteous. It does not regard the proper limits of its own sphere of working, but from its own partial insights would deduce a whole interpretation of reality. Similarly, we all admire the 'catholic spirit'. John Wesley had a famous sermon with that very title, in which he pleaded eloquently for unity on essentials, but charity on non-essentials. 'I believe', he said 'the episcopal form of Church government to be scriptural and apostolic. If you think the Presbyterian or Independent is better, think so still and act accordingly.' This irenic spirit is of the very mind of Christ. But the 'catholic attitude' is a much more hardened and intolerant version of it. It makes unyielding assumptions from inadequate premises, and assumes an authority it has no right to possess. Whilst that intolerant exclusiveness persists, no true progress in Church relations can be made.

The great contemporary need is by conference and discussion to reach certain limited objectives. Membership in any of the Christian Churches ought to carry membership in all. There ought to be mutual recognition of the validity of the orders of Christian Ministers in historic communions so that the pulpit is unfenced. There ought to be inter-Communion so that all who love the Lord Jesus have the right to communicate in any Christian Church in any land wherever the Feast is spread. Both at home (especially in new areas) and in overseas missionary enterprise, there ought to be a unified policy among the Churches to prevent overlapping and to make the best use of men and resources.

These objectives can only be realized when each knows he has his own contribution to bring to the common treasury. This demands open-heartedness and open-mindedness, together with loyalty to one's spiritual heritage. It is the mental attitude which declares: 'I have received a gift from God which I desire to share with you.' There has been a succession of books in recent years on ecumenism but none more important than L. A. Zander's *Vision and Action*. Professor Zander is a member of the Russian Orthodox Church, but his survey shows a sympathetic understanding of the ecumenical problems and opportunities confronting us all. The conclusion of the long and carefully developed argument is that 'in our theological ecumenism, in our joint prayers, in the mystical vision of Christ's image in one another, we somehow grow together in spirit, and there comes to be a new kind of unity which does not annul our divisions but in some way co-exists with them'.[2] The watchword which Professor Zander coins is 'Unity without union'. One need not accept the author's view that this is our final goal, because it might seem unduly despairing of organic union. Nevertheless it is a true and penetrating word which he utters. The immediate objective is not the union of the Churches but the unity of the Church.

We cannot even be certain whether ultimately the Holy Spirit will bring us all into one uniform, organized Church. In Wesley's Conference of 1747 the following two questions and answers were recorded.

Q. Must there not be numberless accidental variations in the government of the various Churches?

A. There must in the nature of things. As God dispenses His gifts of nature, providence, and grace, both the officers and the offices in each ought to be varied from time to time.

Q. Why is there no determinate plan of Church government appointed in Scripture?

A. Without doubt because the wisdom of God had a regard to the necessary variety.

The 'coming great Church', even if it be one, will need to preserve those rich and varied insights with which the separate Churches were endowed by the Holy Spirit.

Meanwhile the present task is not to work for our unity, but to become aware of it. The Churches, in a word, have not to achieve unity, but to express in thought and action a unity which already exists.

[2] Page 217.

It is the Church, holy and apostolic, which the Holy Spirit uses as His main instrument for bringing men to repentance and so into the Kingdom. In this goodly fellowship there is confession and intercession and witness on behalf of all the family of mankind. In the offered prayer, in the reading of the Word, and its interpretation, in the outspread Table, the needs of all men are lifted up to the great Mediator who liveth to make intercession for us. And not only through its worship and its sacraments, but through its apostolic labours, the Church brings men into the fold.

It is to such a Church that the Christian belongs. He takes his place in the goodly fellowship of apostles, prophets, and martyrs. In holding fast the blessed truth of the communion of saints, he knows that the Church on earth and the Church in heaven cannot be divided. As Charles Wesley expressed it:

> *The Church triumphant in Thy love,*
> *Their mighty joys we know;*
> *They sing the Lamb in hymns above,*
> *And we in hymns below.*

> *Thee in Thy glorious realm they praise,*
> *And bow before Thy throne,*
> *We in the Kingdom of Thy grace:*
> *The Kingdoms are but one.*

It was the same Charles Wesley who in vivid metaphor described the fellowship of believers as one Church above, beneath, and as one family with but the narrow stream of death flowing between. But even this stream does not truly divide, for, he says,

> *One army of the Living God,*
> *To His command we bow;*
> *Part of His host have crossed the flood,*
> *And part are crossing now.*

This is the heritage of the Christian. He belongs to the Universal Church which fills both earth and skies. He knows that to that glorious Church have been given the keys of the Kingdom of Heaven, that what it binds on earth shall be bound in heaven, and what it looses on earth, shall be loosed in heaven.

He therefore faces an uncertain future with a certain hope. He knows that the saints are equipped, through the spirit of God, for the work of ministering, for the building up of the body of Christ; till we all attain unto the unity of the faith and of the knowledge of the Son of God. The writer of the Second Epistle of Peter knew that though the heavens and earth would be dissolved, the word of God would not pass away, and in dramatic language he set forth his belief in the sure foundation of God. 'The day of the Lord', he said, 'will come like a thief, when the heavens will vanish with crackling roar, the stars will be set ablaze and melt, the earth and all its works will disappear.' At such an awful time what might a reasonable man anticipate? The writer gives the answer: 'It is new heavens and a new earth that we expect, as He has promised, and in them dwells righteousness. Then, beloved, as you are expecting this, be eager to be found by him unspotted and unblemished in serene assurance' (Moffatt).

That triumphant passage is the note of the New Testament as it is the note of the Christian Church. The house that was built upon the rock could not be shaken by the violence of the storm. And because the Church is founded upon a rock it shall not be moved:

> *In vain the surge's angry shock,*
> *In vain the drifting sands;*
> *Unharmed upon the eternal Rock*
> *The eternal City stands.*

Here then is the sum of the matter. In this period of time between the Resurrection and the Parousia, there is entrusted to the Church on earth, one in spite of its many divisions, the saving word of grace. It proclaims a present Kingdom into which all may enter as they subject themselves to the rule of the King. This Kingdom, as Isaiah prophesied, is established and upheld with justice and with righteousness for ever. We live in days when men seek to recover order in the thinking and conduct of their lives. Here is the very basis of that order, its form and content and significance. Johann Jacob Schültz sang joyously:

> *Within the Kingdom of His might,*
> *Lo! all is just and all is right:*
> *To God all praise and glory.*

And all who will may enter in.

CHAPTER XIII

THE ENEMY IN THE FIELD

THE time rapidly approaches when, though a man cannot serve two masters, he must serve one. We live in a century of fiercely competing ideologies. Stalin, to Western thinking, may have been a blood-thirsty tyrant whose remarkable tenacity and leadership in the war cannot efface the memory of his ruthless drive to power and his cold-blooded use of it. In Stalin's hands Marxist thinking received a new and revolutionary twist. Lenin had already modified his master's teaching by suggesting that emancipation would come through a band of intellectuals rather than through the proletariat itself. He was far more ready than Marx to concede that ideas rather than economic circumstances would precipitate the revolution, and he showed himself ready to use violence to help the revolution onwards. Here was no theory of the 'ripe apple', no waiting for the moment when through its own inner contradictions capitalism would lie wide open to attack. Lenin believed that events could be hastened and history told which way to go.

Stalin went farther. Trotsky, as the faithful disciple of Karl Marx, believed in socialism not for one country but for the world. In his mortal struggle with Trotsky, Stalin developed the dogma of socialism in one country. He rejected the idea that Russia could not achieve Marxian socialism unaided; and by his adulation of Soviet Russia, he was able to harness the mighty power of nationalist emotion. Russia was the true centre of the world, the third Rome, the realized dream of those who thought about the future.

In the execution of this policy, the criticism freely allowed in Lenin's day became high treason. Effective power passed into the hands of one man. The Party Congress had met annually until Lenin's death; the five which met in Stalin's dictatorship did no more than register their approval of his policy when he chose to summon them. Marx had subordinated force to social and economic processes; but in this monolithic Communist State, unhesitating reliance was placed upon the use of force. If men agreed, well and good; but if they opposed you, then they must take the consequences.

Stalin is dead, and though no one leader is clearly in possession, the Russian State as he fashioned and forged it still remains. Steadily it plots its course towards a Marxian goal of history. It profits from the timidity, indecision, and confusion of others. It is strengthened by the staggering advance of Communism in Asia. No country is potentially stronger in men and resources than China, and China accepts the same ideology. India, despite a strong Communist minority, still follows a policy of neutrality; but who would dare to prophesy that the Indian Congress may not one day be under Communist domination? It is true that the ancient world-religions have known in recent years a certain revival; Buddhism seems actually to be on the march. But the momentum of events both in China and South East Asia has shown how easily these Faiths can be set aside.

Communism, with its revolutionary dogmas and its sturdy eschatology, is a fighting faith under which uncounted millions are content to live and for which they are prepared to die. Those who are ready to compromise with its thought forms on the basis of give and take may be prepared for the fate of the young lady of Riga; indisputably there will be a smile on the face of the tiger. There will be periods of greater and of less strain, but the tension will continue.

In such a century, the individual or nation without an alternative system of values and belief must fare ill. Communism must not be regarded as a problem, or even as a threat, but as a challenge. Those who have no adequate philosophy of life and no fixed standard of values can only rely upon opportunism and expediency. They are not enough. The house built on the sand is swept away in the time of storm. The peril of the non-Communist world lies in lack of faith. Unless we know the purpose of living and the destiny of man, our inner emptiness will one day be exposed. Those who last longest in a cold war are those who have the answers to the ultimate questions about the nature of God, of man, and of the Last Things. Nominal Christianity is not enough. The way forward does not lie with Mr By-ends. He said, in John Bunyan's *Pilgrim's Progress:* 'It is true we somewhat differ in religion from those of the stricter sort, yet but in two small points; first, we never strive against wind and tide; secondly, we are most zealous when religion goes in his silver slippers; we love much to talk with him in the street if the sun shines, and the people applaud him.'

There is now both wind and tide, and there are no silver slippers. The convinced Christian is the only fit match for the convinced Marxist; and only the Christian Faith can out-think and out-stay Communism in this fight for the soul of man. The Communist is sustained not only by his present achievements, but by his future prospects. He knows that the goal of history can be reached, that the time process ends in fulfilment. He believes he can afford to wait, and so patience is knit with tenacity.

M

If camp-followers are to become soldiers, if Christians are to be effective, there must be not only an enthusiastic acceptance of present discipline, but a knowledge of the eventual triumph. The implications of three key words need to be accepted. They are Anti-Christ, the Second Coming, and the Final Judgement.

As Reinhold Niebuhr argued in his Gifford Lecture, *The Nature and Destiny of Man*, the symbol of Anti-Christ is best understood as the dramatization of that evil which stands at the end of history. It is therefore a denial of Utopianism, which argues that good will be the final goal of ill, and it refutes the idea that men will emerge from their errors as a butterfly emerges from the chrysalis. No paradise will emerge from the institutions and arrangements of men. Evil cumulates even as the good, and at the end there is both Christ and Anti-Christ.

The issue is supremely set forth by our Lord in the parable of the tares. In recorded history the tares grow with the wheat, and you cannot by education, science, or politics find a method finally to separate them. You cannot straighten the twisted will or exorcise the corruption in human nature. Every fresh generation brings anew the tensions of a divided nature and the fact and consequences of original sin. Once again, as children grow, the Apostle's cry is heard. 'I approve the better I follow the worse.' In every age the tares grow with the wheat. Who can marvel therefore if in the Johannine epistles the Anti-Christ and not the earthly paradise is manifested at the end?

This Christian view of human destiny is a preventive against despair. It never allows us to suppose at the end there will be nothing but the field of golden grain, and so it delivers us from false hopes that can easily mislead. The weakness of Nazi propaganda during the war years was that the people were buoyed up with exaggerated and misleading accounts of German success. Consequently they were quite unfitted to stand the shock of reversal when it came. Once the truth could no longer be hid, the propaganda ministry was entirely discredited and the nation was finally disillusioned. The Christian knowledge of the incessant warfare between good and evil begets a quiet mind and a steadfast purpose.

It also saves us from a false comfort. If history is on our side, as humanists and Communists assert, we can be lulled into an illusory security; we can believe the escalator is always moving. But for the Christian the fight is always on. In every generation there is the struggle against private and public wrong. 'The price of liberty is eternal vigilance,' but so is the price of all things worth defending.

What has been secured so painfully can so easily be lost. The sword therefore must not sleep in the hand. Ours will never be the satisfaction of final victory; it is not given to the soldiers to drive the enemy from the field. As Reinhold Niebuhr has said: 'The Antichrist who appears at the end of history can be defeated only by the Christ who ends history.' Nevertheless we have the zest of fighting for the Kingdom in an army terrible with banners. By our work men are brought into the Kingdom and so the Kingdom advances in the hearts of men.

Finally we are delivered from a false confidence. Our trust is never in man to deliver himself, but only in the Lord of the harvest who will see that the grain is not lost. There will, said Jesus, be the time of harvest, and in that day the tares will be separated from the wheat. The good will not be lost; Truth will not be overthrown. We are the labourers, but our labour will not be in vain in the Lord.

The guarantee of this sure confidence is in the eschatological symbol of the Parousia. The Lord will come again. Every student of the Last Things is indebted to Dr T. F. Glasson, who in his books on the Second Advent has discounted on biblical grounds the idea of a literal second appearance of our Lord. Even so, it is unwise to substitute for the Parousia the fourth Gospel's teaching on the activity of the Holy Spirit. Most certainly we are brought by His aid to recognize that reward is associated with goodness and frustration with wrong-doing. So, by trial and error, men are brought to see that it is only in God's way that they can walk without stumbling. Through His work in the individual heart, in the Church, and in the world, the Holy Spirit guides us into all the truth. The Bible however forbids us to think that in a space-time order this process of teaching will ever be perfected.

The Kingdom did not begin with man, nor by man can it be consummated; the Author and Perfecter is God. Because we refuse to take refuge in a crude literalism, we must not dismiss the truth behind apocalyptic imagery. Of that day and hour no one knows, not the angels, not even the Son of Man. But God knows, and in His own time and in His own manner He will consummate all things. In God's subjection of all to Himself, there will be made evident His power and majesty. Immanentism is a soft-sounding word that goes easily with pantheism; it needs the corrective of transcendentalism to give it substance. The transcendental God is not only 'the wisdom and the energy that fills the world with power'; He is the active Ruler catastrophically intervening in the great crises of history. We need the similitude of the leaven and the mustard seed to describe His working, but also the conception of the Lord on the clouds of glory. Only the God who is above can rescue those who are beneath.

> *The God that rules on high,*
> *That all the earth surveys,*
> *That rides upon the stormy sky,*
> *And calms the roaring seas:*
> *This awful God is ours,*
> *Our Father and our love;*
> *He will send down His heavenly powers,*
> *To carry us above.*

This end of history is not to be pictured as the eventual victory of God after protracted warfare on earth. The Gospel emblazons the truth that God is already triumphant; His glory now fills the heavens. But at the Parousia all men shall see His glory and acknowledge His rule. Then Isaiah's prophecy will have a new significance: 'unto me every knee shall bow, every tongue shall swear. Only in the Lord shall one say unto me is righteousness and strength: even to Him shall men come, and all that were incensed against Him shall be ashamed.'

The third great symbol of the eschata or last things is the Final Judgement. No truth could express more powerfully the fact that we live in a moral order and we shall be judged as moral beings. Seedtime and harvest only exemplify in nature what is true also in human nature. 'Be not deceived; God is not mocked: for whatsoever a man soweth, that shall he also reap.' The judgement proceeds in time. Although God sent His Son not to judge the world but to save the world, men are judged by their treatment of the Son. To believe is not to be judged, but to believe not is to be judged already. John's Gospel emphasizes the principle of judgement. If light is come and men prefer darkness rather than light, then their judgement is unto condemnation. If men love the light and walk in the light, their judgement is unto reward.

So understood, we pass a present judgement upon all our thoughts and words and action. The oft-recorded story of the self-opinionated lady criticizing the masterpiece in an art gallery has its relevance. The guide listened to the vulgar outpouring and then said quietly: 'Madam, you do not judge the picture; the picture judges you.'

By the attitude we take to our own conscience, by our attitude to others, and supremely by our attitude to God, we are judged already. And the judgement is unto reward or condemnation, unto life or death. Paul's whole treatment of the law was based on the fact that it brought knowledge of right and wrong, and therefore disobedience was conscious.

There is no blame for the small child who tells 'whoppers' innocently, or whose straying fingers refuse to distinguish between other people's property and his own. Once, however, he arrives at the state of knowledge between mine and thine, right and wrong, truth and falsehood, he is under judgement. According to the light we have received, we are continually being judged. Toynbee has shown that on a large scale the judgement is passed on nations, empires, and civilizations. In our own century we have had leisure to reflect upon the nemesis of totalitarian systems whose gods were false gods. Whenever nations deny the true God and turn aside to idols, their wrong system of values destroys them. Soon or late, their doom is writ. This is just as true of individuals. To defy God's purpose and to choose one's own way is to stand in an outer darkness where sooner or later can be heard wailing and the gnashing of teeth.

The *Te Deum*, which has been the possession of the whole Church for sixteen centuries, is theology set to music, and in it is nobly set forth the whole work of Christ. Certain key phrases indicate stages in the divine drama: the virgin's womb, the sharpness of death, the opening of the Kingdom of Heaven, sitting on the right hand of God. Here in staccato language is the Incarnation, the Crucifixion, the Resurrection, and the Ascension. But the end is not yet. The ascended Lord has another office to fulfil:

We believe that Thou shalt come to be our Judge.

Augustine detected a certain significance in this judgement by the Son rather than the Father, and argued that as He was judged by the world, so the world must be judged by Him. We shall be judged by what we have made of His life and teaching according to the opportunities given to us.

To many the very idea of judgement seems inconsistent with the revelation of God as love. But in time as well as eternity, is it not heaven to respond to love and hell to reject it? The Parable of the Prodigal Son is a story with a happy end. Before it was too late, the son recognized the value of the gift he had contemptuously spurned. Even the hired servants in the Father's house seemed incomparably more blessed than himself. He had become involved in a hell which he devised for himself when he sinfully rejected the father's love. But supposing he had stayed in the far country—how great would have been his loss. The father would have been waiting, and in the son's very refusal to return, judgement would have been passed. 'If the light that is in thee be darkness, how great is the darkness.'

The fact of a moral order demands that according to the sowing there shall be the reaping. A man can only behave with impunity in an amoral universe. Where there is a cosmic purposelessness there need be, apart from expediency, no human purpose; a man may do as he wishes. But in God's universe even God cannot break His own order. Judgement there must be even though the Judge bears wound-prints in His hands.

Indeed the direct words on moral responsibility were spoken by the 'gentle Jesus, meek and mild'. Who told the frightening story of Dives and Lazarus? Who spoke of the narrow way leading to life and the broad way leading to destruction? Who spoke of sheep and goats and their separate destinies? Who uttered the words, 'Inasmuch as ye did it not. . . .'?

There came in the nineteenth century a reaction against the older teaching on hell-fire. 'It is an offence against the God we see in Jesus Christ,' men cried. They argued that the mind cannot hold in the same sweep of imagining a lonely figure on a cross and a lonely soul in torment. Quite rightly the literalism of fire and brimstone was rejected. But soon even fires of remorse and unatoned guilt seemed highly-drawn and emotional. We threw away the picture with the picture frame. We did not realize that if hell goes, then sooner or later heaven follows suit.

It did not occur to us that if we discount judgement we deny the morality of the world and its Ruler. We did not realize that if we are responsible, we are also accountable, and that the Judgement Seat of God dramatizes the truth that we are not mice but men. Just because we are not puppets with no will of our own, we can determine our habits, our life, and our destiny. There is the ceaseless pursuit of the Hound of Heaven; there are the thousand importunities of the Divine lover; but in the end we choose the way to go. The Day of Judgement safeguards the truth of man's dignity as a son of God who makes his heaven or hell. It acknowledges his status even as it speaks its warning.

But all that escaped us. Material prosperity had softened our spiritual fibre. We sentimentalized the idea of God and forfeited our biblical inheritance. It became difficult enough to believe in the resurrection of the dead, and impossible to believe in the conception of Judgement. Phrases such as 'it doesn't matter what you believe' kept company with 'we're all going to the same place'. Omar Khay-yám had remarkable popularity: 'Pish! he's a good fellow' and ' 'twill all be well'. We believed with Heine that God would forgive; '*C*'*est son métier.*'

In this century, however, we have had two World Wars, and the prospect of a third is a prospect of world annihilation. Events have driven us out of the old security. Theology sounds a more sombre note. We have rediscovered both the depth in God and the depth in man. We have been forced to believe in Judgement, because we have seen it in operation. Having seen, however fitfully, we can no longer be the same again. We live in apocalyptic days, and the God who was a Victorian grandfather has gone for ever. If there is judgement here and now, why may there not equally be judgement here and here-after? At least we know it is not seemly to acknowledge the fact and dispute the duration. Nor is it proper in the light of our chastening experience to trespass on the indulgence of a loving Father. If the dominical words on Judgement are to be taken seriously, then God must be taken seriously. All error creeps in when there is error in thinking about God.

The twenty-fifth chapter of Matthew has a contemporary applica-tion. It speaks of the unfortunates who forfeit bliss. This is not a gallery of rogues, but of decent people who misunderstood the nature of God. There were some nice girls who were only foolish, a thrifty man whom no Police Officer could convict, and finally some well-intentioned people who thought they were on excellent terms with God. How did they come to blunder so tragically?—They had a wrong idea of God.

Consider the case of the foolish virgins. They believed the bride-groom to be pleasant, tolerant, and easy-going. They could do what they liked with their time and he would understand. So they wasted their time and he came when they were absent. They returned to find the door shut and their cries unavailing. Those who waste their days, content in their unpreparedness, find at last the Bridegroom is other than they think.

Then Jesus spoke of the thrifty man who did not like his master and so refused to serve Him. The childish pictures of God as the almighty school-master fill the minds of many throughout their lives. He is the dark Opposite, the to-be-feared Unknown, the Judge without compassion. They believe, but they do not love or understand. 'Curse God and die,' said Job's wife, and many would agree. Think-ing of God in that fashion, they hoard their gift. Too late they find that in spiting God they have only hurt themselves. Narrow thoughts of God mean constriction of living; large thoughts of God mean abundance of life.

Then Jesus spoke of the people with the patter. In Sutton Vane's play *Outward Bound*, the celestial inspector who comes on board is wearing a clerical collar. Many suppose that God has not only a special interest in denominations but in their techniques. They are deluded into supposing that because their feelings about Him are entirely cosy and the language they use is entirely suitable, they will be acknowledged by Him at once. If their patter is somewhat 'phoney', their cry of astonishment at His denial of them is genuine and alarmed.

It is right to speak of God as the good shepherd, so long as we know He is also a consuming fire. It is good to know that underneath are the everlasting arms, so long as we also realize that 'it is a fearful thing to fall into the hands of the living God'. Despite the grim warnings of this century of blood, we are still in danger of not discerning the signs of the times. Because we refuse to take Him with utmost seriousness, we discount the gravity of His words. We do not live therefore as those who must stand before the Judgement Seat of God. We can be careless, or petulant, or self-deceiving, but in the Parables the fate of all such people was the same.

If in the gathering momentum of events we refuse to take heed, if we refuse to work whilst the day lasts and the night tarries, then shall be heard again that awful sentence: 'I say unto you it shall be more tolerable for Tyre and Sidon in the day of judgement than for you.'

Before that sentence of doom is delivered there is the swiftly passing moment. It brings a promise and an exhortation. 'Awake, thou that sleepest, and arise from the dead, and Christ shall shine upon thee.' Judgement stands, but it can be a judgement unto life. Faithfulness is all. Those who know that they will meet Him as Judge will greet Him as Lord.

SELECT BIBLIOGRAPHY

ONCE I commented upon a book that it moved somewhat sluggishly between the high banks of references. I have wanted to avoid that same fault and perhaps have thereby laid myself open to the counter charge. Maybe I have not given the reader sufficient footnotes. A writer can be too sparing as well as too prodigal. In his desire for readers to follow with minimum distraction the flow of the narrative, he may cause some to be impeded in their reading by the very fact that authorities have not been quoted.

Lest this should happen here, I want to indicate in a short bibliography the books which have been of direct assistance to me in my task. At the same time the reader will understand my larger indebtedness to very many writers who may not have immediately influenced my writing of this particular book, but who have helped to furnish my mind throughout the years so that I cannot even begin to assess a debt as high as a mountain. There can, for example, be no attempt to catalogue works of the great political philosophers, nor general histories, nor biblical nor theological works other than those I have needed in the writing of this book. It was only against the background of that wider reading that I was able to approach the task at all.

Here then follows a list of selected books:

SECTION I

AGAR, HERBERT, *Declaration on Faith*, 1952.

BAINTON, R. H., *Here I Stand* (Life of Martin Luther), 1950.

CANHAM, E., *The World at Mid-century*, 1950.

DAWSON, CHRISTOPHER, *Understanding Europe*, 1952.

*DE BEUS, J. S., *The Future of the West*, 1954.

DIXON, W. MACNEILE, *The Human Situation*, 1938.

GREEN, N. H. H., *Renaissance and Reformation*, 1952.

HILDEBRANDT, FRANZ, *From Luther to Wesley*, 1951.

LIPPMAN, WALTER, *A Preface to Morals*, 1931.

*LUBAC, HENRI, *Drama of Atheist Humanism*, 1949.

MURDOCH, IRIS, *Jean Paul Sartre—The Romantic Rationalist*, 1953.

ROLT, L. T. C., *High Horse Riderless*, 1947.

RUPP, GORDON, *The Righteousness of God*, 1953.

SARTRE, JEAN PAUL, *Literary and Philosophical Essays*, 1955.

*TAWNEY, R. H., *Religion and the Rise of Capitalism*, 1938.

WATSON, P., *The State as the Servant of God*, 1946; *Let God be God*, 1947.

WHALE, J. S., *The Protestant Tradition*, 1955.

*WOOD, H. G., *Belief and Unbelief since 1850*, 1955.

SECTION II

BARKER, ERNEST, *Change and Continuity*, 1949.

BRUNNER, EMIL, *Justice and the Social Order*, 1945.

COLE, G. D. H., *Essays on Social Theory*, 1950.

*DICEY, A. V., *Law and Opinion in England*, 1920.

ELIOT, T. S., *The Idea of a Christian Society*, 1939.

FASNACHT, *Lord Acton on Nationality and Socialism*, 1949.

GILBY, THOS., *Between Community and Society*, 1953.

JONES, G. VAUGHAN, *Democracy and Civilization*, 1947.

LOFTHOUSE, W. F., *F. H. Bradley*, 1949.

LOWRY, C. W., *Communism and Christ*, 1954.

MACIVER, R. M., *The Web of Government*, 1947.

MURRAY, R. A., *History of Political Science*, 1926.

NEEDHAM, JOS., *History is on Our Side*, 1946.

ORWELL, GEORGE, *Animal Farm*, 1948; *Nineteen Eighty-four*, 1949.

ORR, LORD BOYD, *Science, Politics and Peace*, 1950.

PACKE, MICHAEL, *The Life of John Stuart Mill*, 1954.

ROGERS, EDWARD, *Commentary on Communism*, 1951.

SCHAPIRO, J. S., *World in Crisis*, 1950.

SCHUMPETER, J. A., *Capitalism, Socialism and Democracy*, 1947.

THOULLESS, R. H., *Authority and Freedom*, 1952.

*WAYPER, C. L., *Political Thought*, 1954.

SECTION III

ADLER, ALFRED, *Understanding Human Nature*, 1937.

BAUR, J. I., *Revolution and Tradition in Modern American Art*, 1951.

BLANSHARD, F. B., *Retreat from Likeness in the theory of Painting*, 1949.

*BLOCH, MARC, *The Historian's Craft*, 1954.

BROAD, C. D., *Religion, Philosophy and Psychical Research*, 1953.

BROWN, J. A. C., *The Social Psychology of Industry*, 1954.

BROWN, W., *Psychology and Psychotherapy*, 1934.

BROWN, W. B. D., & RAPHAEL, W., *Managers, Men and Morale*, 1948.

BUMMARTEN, F., *Psychology of Human Relations in Industry*, 1950.

BURNHAM, JAMES, *The Managerial Revolution*, 1945.

*BUTTERFIELD, HERBERT, *History of Human Relations*, 1951; *Christianity and History*, 1949; *Origins of Modern Science*, 1949; *Christianity, Diplomacy and War*, 1953.

CALDER, R., *Man v. The Desert*, 1951.

CARR, E. H., *The Twenty Years Crisis (1919–39)*, 1946.

CARREL, ALEXIS, *Man the Unknown*, 1948.

CASEY, R. S., *Double or Quit (Industrial Relations)*, 1949.

CONANT, J. B., *Modern Science and Modern Man*, 1952.

COULSON, C. A., *Science and Christian Belief*, 1955.

DEMUTH, NORMAN, *Musical Trends in the Twentieth Century*, 1952.

DEVANEY, JAMES, *Poetry in Our Time*, 1952.

*DINGLE, HERBERT, *The Scientific Adventure*, 1952.

ENGLISH, RAYMOND, *Pursuit of Purpose*, 1947.

EWERS, J. K., *Creative Writing in Australia*, 1945.

EYSENCK, H. J., *The Uses and Abuses of Psychology*, 1953.

FASNACHT, S. E., *Acton's Political Philosophy*, 1952.

*FOLLETT, MARY PARKER, *Dynamic Administration*, 1941.

*FRASER, G. S., *The Modern Writer and his World*, 1953.

GHISELLI, E. E., & BROWN, C. W., *Personnel and Industrial Psychology*, 1948.

GINSBERG, M., *Reason and Unreason in Society*, 1947.

GORDON, STRATHEARN, *A People's Conscience*, 1952.

HEATH, H. E., ed., *Scientific Thought in the Twentieth Century*, 1951.

HEDDIE, ENID, *Australian Literature Now*, 1945.

HOYLE, FRED, *A Decade of Decision*, 1953.

HUTSCHRECKER, A. A., *The Will to Live*, 1952.

HYAMS, ED., *Soil, and Civilization*, 1952.

JACKS, G. V., & WHYTE, R. O., *The Rape of the Earth*, 1939.

JASPERS, K., *Origin and Goal of History*, 1949.

JESSOP, T. E., *Social Ethics: Christian and Natural*, 1952.

JOHNSON, MARTIN, *Art and Scientific Thought*.

JUENGER, F. S., *The Failure of Technology*, 1949.

*JUNG, C. G., *Modern Man in Search of a Soul*, 1936.

KLINBANSKY & PATON, A., *Philosophy and History*.

LIEBMAN, J. L., *Peace of Mind*, 1946.

LINDSAY, A. D., *Religion, Science and Society in the Modern World*, 1943.

LEWIS, WYNDHAM, *The Demon of Progress in the Arts*, 1954.

LEWIS, R., & MAUDE, A., *The English Middle Classes*, 1949.

LIPPMAN, W., *The Good Society*, 1943.

*MANNHEIM, KARL, *Essays on Society and Social Psychology*, 1953.

MAYO, ELTON, *Social Problems of an Industrial Civilization*, 1949.

McKELLAR, PETER, *Text Book of Human Psychology*, 1952.

McNEILL, W., *Past and Future (Chicago, n.d.)*.

MOTTRAM, W. H., *The Philosophical Basis of Personality*, 1944.

OVERSTREET, H. A., *The Great Enterprise*, 1953.

PARKE, W. H., *Salvation Without Saviours*, 1951.

*PIEPER, JOSEF, *Leisure—the Basis of Culture*, 1952.

POLANYI, M., *Science, Faith and Society*, 1946.

PRONKO, A. H., ed., *Empirical Foundations of Psychology*, 1953.

RAVEN, C. E., *Science, Religion and the Future*, 1943; *Science and the Christian Man*, 1952.

*RAVEN, C. E., *Natural Religion and Christian Theology* (2 vols.), 1953.

READ, HERBERT, *Philosophy of Modern Art*, 1952.

RENIER, J. G., *History: Its Purpose and Method*, 1950.

*RUSSELL, BERTRAND, *History of Western Philosophy*, 1946.

*SEARS, PAUL B., *Deserts on the March*, 1949.

SEERBOHM, ROWNTREE & LAVERS, G. R., *English Life and Leisure*, 1951.

SHERWOOD TAYLOR, F., *A Century of Science*, 1941.

SMITH, C. R., *The Mind and the Universe*, 1954.

SMUTTS, J. C., *Holism and Evolution*, 1926.

*SOKOLOFF, BORIS, *Science and the Purpose of Life*, 1950.

SOROKIN, P.A., *Social and Cultural Dynamics* (3 vols.), 1937; *Social Philosophies of an Age of Crisis*, 1953.

SOAL, S. G., & BATEMAN, F., *Modern Experiments in Telepathy*, 1954.

SPROTT, W. J., *Social Psychology*, 1952.

STEBBING, SUSAN, *Philosophy and the Physicists*, 1944.

THOULESS, R. H., *Psychical Research Past and Present*, 1952.

TOYNBEE, ARNOLD, *The Study of History: The World and the West*, 1953.

TYRRELL, G. N. M., *The Personality of Man*, 1946.

UNAMUNO, MIGUEL DE, *The Tragic Sense of Life*, 1931.

*VOGT, WILLIAM, *Road to Survival*, 1949.

*WALKER, KENNETH, *Meaning and Purpose*, 1944.

WALTER, W. GREY, *The Living Brain*, 1952.

WATSON, O. L., *The Study of Human Nature*, 1953.

*WALTON, A., *Fundamentals of Industrial Psychology*, 1941.

WEBB, W. PRESCOTT, *The Great Frontier*, 1953.

WORDSWORTH, R. S., *Contemporary Schools of Psychical Research*, 1951.

YOUNG, J. Z., *Doubt and Certainty in Science*, 1950.

ZANGWILL, O. L., *Introduction to Modern Psychology*, 1950.

*ZEHRER, HANS, *Man in this World*, 1952.

ZWEIG, F., *The British Worker*, 1952.

SECTION IV

BAILLIE, D. M., *God was in Christ*, 1948.

BAILLIE, JOHN, *What is Christian Civilization?*, 1947.

*BERDYAEV, N., *The Destiny of Man*, 1937.

BRUNNER, EMIL, *The Mediator*, 1947.

*CAIRNS, DAVID, *Image of God in Man*, 1953.

*CAVE, SYDNEY, *The Christian Estimate of Man*, 1944.

CRAIG, C. T., *The One Church*, 1952.

DAVIES, HORTON, *The English Free Churches*, 1952.

DICKIE, J., *Fifty Years of British Theology*, 1953.

DILLISTONE, F. W., *The Structure of the Divine Society*, 1951.

DODD, C. H., *The Parables of the Kingdom*, 1936; *The Apostolic Preaching and its Developments*, 1936; *History and the Gospel*, 1938.

FERRÉ, NELS, *The Christian Understanding of God*, 1951.

FLEW, R. NEWTON, *Jesus and His Church*, 1943.

GREENSLADE, S. L., *The Church and Social Order*, 1948.

HEBERT, A. G., *The Form of the Church*, 1944.

*HOPPER, S. R., *The Crisis of Faith*, 1941.

JORDON, E. K. H., *Free Church Unity*, 1956.

JENKINS, DANIEL T., *The Gift of Ministry*, 1947.

*MARITAIN, JACQUES, *The Range of Reason*, 1953.

MANSON, T. W., *The Church's Ministry*, 1948; *The Sayings of Jesus*, 1949.

MOUVOUX, JEAN, *The Meaning of Man*, 1948.

*NIEBUHR, REINHOLD, *Nature and Destiny of Man* (2 vols.), 1941; *Faith and History*, 1949.

NELSON, J. R., *The Realm of Redemption*, 1951.

PAUL, LESLIE, *The Meaning of Human Existence*, 1949.

RECKITT, M. B., *Maurice to Temple*, 1947.

ROBERTS, HAROLD, *Jesus and the Kingdom of God*, 1955.

*ROBINSON, WILLIAM, *Whither Theology*, 1953.

SANGSTER, W. E., *The Pure in Heart*, 1954.

THE FRONTIER, Vol. 1 (1950), Vol. 2 (1951), Vol. 3 (1952).

VIDLER, ALEC R., *Christian Belief*, 1950.

WEIL, SIMONE, *The Need for Roots*, 1952.

*ZANDER, L. A., *Vision and Action*, 1952.

Certain books have been found useful in more than one section, but I have listed them only once. Those books marked with an asterisk I have found specially useful for my purpose.

INDEX